MW00765014

EDITOR
Cynthia Davidson

PROTAGONISTS
Denise Bratton
Catherine Ingraham
Julie Rose
R.E. Somol
Sarah Whiting

INTERNS
Benjamin Kroll
Sam Woodworth

PROOFREADERS
Larissa Babij
Sam Woodworth

DESIGN CONSULTANT
Michael Bierut

LOG RENDERER
Wes Jones

WEB DESIGNER
Scott Valins

VERY GOOD FRIENDS WHOSE HELP MAKES LOG POSSIBLE
Anonymous
Eisenman Architects
Charles Gwathmey
Elise Jaffe & Jeffrey Brown
SOM Foundation
Rodney and Susan Wagner

Published by the Anyone Corporation, a
not-for-profit corporation in the State of
New York with editorial and business
offices at:
41 West 25th Street, 11th fl.
New York, New York 10010
Tel: 212-645-1400
Fax: 212-645-0726
Email: log@anycorp.com
Web: www.anycorp.com
ISSN: 1547-4690
ISBN: 0-9746521-1-3
Printed in the USA.

Log is no eclogue, no pastoral poem, that is, but a chronology of sorts, a record of some observations made in our time. Hence it may be useful to situate publication of *Log* 2 in the context of recent events. Events such as the heralded opening of Frank Gehry's swoop-of-silver Disney Concert Hall (we remember when, back in 1991, pre-Bilbao, it was to be clad in stone) and the less well-received unveiling of Gehry's design for a new Stanley Cup (for those who don't follow sports, that's the championship trophy awarded each spring in the National Hockey League). We mention these because, to date, neither is mentioned by contributors to *Log*, and we wonder why. The work of Rem Koolhaas, on the other hand, is the subject of several *Log* entries (about which one could ask why again), including the opening of the McCormick Center at IIT, but not (yet) the opening of the Dutch embassy in Berlin. This past spring there was also the much talked about film, *My Architect*, made by Nathaniel Kahn about his father Louis. If we had a dollar for every time we were asked "Did you see *My Architect*?" we could pay to print this issue. We suspect, however, that architecture wasn't the star of the picture; rather, the pursuit of Kahn-the-absent-father provided the emotional narrative needed to rivet public attention. Structure without narrative is never enough today. And building in India is passé, as China is recruiting more and more Western architects to participate in its building boom and (allegedly) driving up the price of steel with its construction demands. In New York, the Childs/Libeskind disputes over the Freedom Tower faded from the headlines as developers recruited Norman Foster and Jean Nouvel for Ground Zero towers and other Europeans for a 2012 Olympic village design competition. Fumihiko Maki won the competition to renovate the United Nations and a commission for a Ground Zero tower too. The dean searches for architecture departments at Columbia, Cornell, and Harvard also proceeded apace. Lest we forget, amid all the expansion there was also explosion – in Madrid, in Baghdad and Fallujah, in Chechnya, in the Gaza Strip. In the history of war, explosion eventually leads to rebuilding. In Berlin today, racks of postcards featuring the bombed-out and then divided city seem oddly nostaglic alongside the new glaze of Potsdamer Platz. Perhaps the old photographs simply romanticize a time when "the enemy" was clearly defined. As architects pass through metal detectors to hop another plane to the next building site, as ideas migrate from continent to continent, the need to write, and remember, remains.

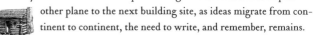

Single copy price: $10.00 US. *Log* is distributed in North America and Asia by the Anyone Corporation and in Europe by Idea Books in Holland. Retailers are encouraged to contact log@anycorp.com for wholesale ordering information or to refer to our web site at www.anycorp.com.

This second issue is being released in June 2004; the third will be published in September 2004. Henceforth, *Log* will be published three times a year. Individuals wishing to receive *Log* in the mail can obtain an annual subscription for $26.00 US (checks only, no credit cards) providing they have a U.S. mailing address. Overseas subscriptions are sent via air mail only, which is an additional $10 fee, for a total subscription cost of $36.00 US (checks must be drawn on US banks). Send cards and letters and subscriptions to our land address. Manuscript submissions may be sent via email or by postal service.

Log

Spring 2004

Observations on architecture and the contemporary city

Cover Story: Toying with Us
Postcard photo by Judith Turner

2

Log *welcomes your comments. Send your cards and letters to 41 West 25th Street, 11th floor, New York, NY 10010; your emails to log@anycorp.com.*

Dear Log:

There was much to think about in Luis Fernández-Galiano's relatively short essay, "Asia on the One Hand, Europe on the Other." I hope it doesn't appear that I disagree with any of his analyses if I correct a small but significant detail. As one of the preliminary jurors in the design competition for the site of the former World Trade Center towers, the absence of any submission of materials from Rem Koolhaas was indeed conspicuous. A number of us on the jury asked that the organizers call his office to see if materials might have been lost in transit but they were informed that OMA was not participating. Many of us wished that they had. In any event, it is not correct to suggest that Koolhaas was "excluded" from the competition.

Terence Riley, The Philip Johnson Chief Curator
The Museum of Modern Art

Dear Log:

It's wonderful to have a new journal of energetic thinking about architecture and its cultural surround. I do, however, want to question Cynthia Davidson's assertion in *Log* 1 that, with the ceasing of publication of *ANY* and *Assemblage*, North America was left "without an open forum for the discussion of contemporary issues in architecture, the making of cities, and all of the cultural asides – political, economic, and otherwise – that architecture and cities engage. In other words, without a platform for criticism and ideas." Is this a parochial or coterie perspective? Are *Perspecta, Harvard Design Magazine, Grey Room, Metropolis,* and even *Architectural Record* chopped liver?

The publication I edit, *Harvard Design Magazine*, is precisely an issue-centered periodical structured for strong debate, criticism, and ideas (one that has, incidentally, published writing by two of *Log*'s first contributors, and that in its current issue publishes an essay by Sanford Kwinter, a regular contributor to *ANY* and *Assemblage*). Is its invisibility to *Log* (and *Log* readers?) a result of its deliberate inclusion of ideologically differing viewpoints? The more commercial *Metropolis* and *Architectural Record* have in recent years been culturally important for publishing bold critiques by people like Michael Sorkin and Joan Ockman.

I wish *Log* well in its effort to be "an open forum," which implies making a special effort to include strong thinking opposed to that of its editors. "Strength seeks fierce criticism to achieve greater strength." – pseudo-Chinese proverb.

William S. Saunders, Editor, *Harvard Design Magazine*

Architekturzentrum Wien

Any Corporation
Cynthia C Davidson
41 West 25th Street, 11th Floor
New York N.Y. 10010

Wien, 22.03.2004

Is Villa Tugendhat about to be destroyed? Open letter to the Mayor of Brno

Dear Mrs. Davidson,

The recent competition for the renovation of Ludwig Mies van der Rohe's Villa Tugendhat and the announcement of the winning firm, combined with what we know of the latter, mean that the original substance of one of the major works of modern architecture is under immanent threat of destruction. In collaboration with the architecture historian Stephan Templ, the Architekturzentrum Wien has written an open letter to the Mayor of Brno. This letter is also an appeal to architects, architecture historians, culture producers and institutions around the world to provide their support.

Please support our appeal!
Enclosed you will find a copy of an open letter to the Mayor of Brno – also available as a download from our homepage at www.azw.at. If you intend to send your own appeal to the Mayor of Brno please send us a copy of your letter.

With kind regards
Dietmar Steiner

Museumsplatz 1
A-1070 Wien
T++43-1-522 31 15
F++43-1-522 31 17
office@azw.at
www.azw.at

No sooner is one historic Mies house saved than another appears to be endangered, or so it seems in recent months (see page 31). Does redevelopment mean modernism has become an artifact? Will a house on the auction block – say a Mies, Corb, or Rietveld – ever fetch the millions that a Picasso just did? Will architecture ever be seen to have a similar artistic value? Stay tuned – or write to the mayor of Brno. – The Log Team

OLAFUR ELIASSON, *THE WEATHER PROJECT*, THE TATE MODERN. OCTOBER 16, 2003 – MARCH 21, 2004. PHOTO: JONAH LOWENFELD.

The Weather Project, *installed in the Turbine Hall of London's Tate Modern Gallery by the Danish artist Olafur Eliasson this past winter, had little to do with the weather per se. The installation was simple, but its effect was profound: Eliasson turned the hall into a 500-foot-long, 75-foot-wide, 115-foot-high black box, with a dropped ceiling of mirrored panels running its length. At the far end, a translucent semicircular scrim diffused the light of hundreds of monofrequency lamps (think highway lights) that hung behind it. Where the scrim met the ceiling, the semicircle and its mirror image became a yellow-orange "sun," the visual center of the work.*

The Weather Project *was even more remarkable for those who knew the Turbine Hall as it was (and is again): a light, airy, often noisy, somewhat blank space. Eliasson transformed it into a dark, meditative chamber. The mirrors that created the sun also doubled the height of the hall, allowing one to see one's own reflection from effectively 24 stories away. Unprompted, many visitors lay on their backs, looking up at themselves. Some groups made words or shapes with their bodies, others did yoga — the "sun salutation" sequence, of course.*

The project captured the imagination of London in winter, attracting one million visitors in its first three months. This had little to do with the phenomenological aspects of Eliasson's work. People came because of the way the space worked on them. While Tate architects Herzog & de Meuron have called the space a "covered street," for five months it was a naturalistic abstraction of a cathedral: deep, towering, narrow, dark, and cold. All gazes were directed toward the golden illumination at the end of the nave, but eventually the visitor moved on to self-reflection. As such, the work defied the artist's intentions and exceeded his expectations.

During the closing weekend of the installation, the Turbine Hall stayed open until midnight on Friday and Saturday. On Sunday, March 21, when the sun went down and the lights came up, the last of the estimated 2.3 million viewers applauded.

— Jonah Lowenfeld

Todd Gannon

The Shape of Things to Come

When dealing with fortune tellers and soothsayers, one should always maintain a degree of suspicion. No matter how much we may want to believe what we're told, deep down we all know it's a scam. Indeed, the best fortune tellers don't predict anything at all – they simply tell us what we already know. Nonetheless we keep coming back, knowing full well that if we are not careful, we are certain to be ripped off.

"The Shape of Things to Come" was held January 16–17, 2004. It was organized by the Austin E. Knowlton School of Architecture at Ohio State University, in association with the Wexner Center for the Arts.

Inviting Peter Eisenman, along with six younger practitioners and a distinguished panel of critics, to the black box theater in Eisenman's own Wexner Center for the Arts, Jeffrey Kipnis focused his crystal ball on "The Shape of Things to Come." Despite its prophetic title, the two-day conference offered little insight on possible futures. It did, however, elucidate the shape of contemporary discourse. Kipnis introduced the event as follows:

The "Shape of Things to Come" conference is convened to honor the long-deferred publication of Peter Eisenman's ground-breaking study, Giuseppe Terragni: Transformations, Decompositions, Critiques, *and his forty-year fixation on the intellectual possibilities of architectural form. In one way or the other, each of the conference participants began their career in Eisenman's sway, then each went on to develop original contributions to the problem of architectural form in his or her own right. Some advanced his research, others redirected it, while others still began to raise doubts about its basic premises. Given the dramatic upheavals in technology, material sciences, and intellectual/cultural discourse that distinguish our world fundamentally from the one in which the contemporary views of architectural form first emerged, The Knowlton School of Architecture convenes the conference to take stock of form, to assess its powers and limitations, and to speculate on its remaining relevance and possible futures, if any.*

Though Eisenman's Terragni book was barely mentioned (leading many in attendance to wonder, owing to the book's infamous difficulty, how many of the participants had actually read it), its specter was present throughout.[1] The complex operational procedures that drove Eisenman's intricate analyses of the Italian modernist permeate his own work as well as that of the architects featured at the conference –

1. At least one participant did read the work. See Sanford Kwinter's excellent review: "Kaddish (for an Architecture Not Born): Peter Eisenman's Giuseppe Terragni," *Bookforum* (Winter 2003): 13–16.

THE PRIZE FOR THE BEST ARCHITEC-
TURE CONFERENCE ANNOUNCEMENT
OF 2004 ARGUABLY GOES TO JEFFREY
KIPNIS AND CREW AT OHIO STATE.

8

2. Alejandro Zaera-Polo was invited as well, but cancelled at the last minute.
3. The conference was organized with a keynote address from Eisenman on Friday night, and presentations from the five invited architects and two panel discussions on Saturday. The three critics did not present but did participate in both panel discussions.
4. An important exception is Jeffrey Kipnis's 1999 exhibition "Perfect Acts of Architecture," which featured works by Eisenman, Rem Koolhaas, Bernard Tschumi, Thom Mayne, and Daniel Libeskind. See the exhibition catalogue *Perfect Acts of Architecture* (New York: Museum of Modern Art, 1999).

Greg Lynn, Wes Jones, Lindy Roy, Thomas Leeser, and Preston Scott Cohen.[2] The significance of those operations has been examined extensively by Kipnis as well as by the two invited critics, Sanford Kwinter and R. E. Somol.[3]

Eisenman began with an extended monologue on "the future of the history of architecture" followed by the presentation of two projects, one he termed "analog," the other "digital"; the former his soon-to-be-completed Memorial to the Murdered Jews of Europe in Berlin and the latter an unrealized train station design for Naples, Italy. By categorizing the projects in these terms, Eisenman implied a technical divide between the by-hand techniques employed by his own generation and the computer-driven methodologies that currently dominate the discipline. Given the hegemony of digital techniques over all the conference participants (including Eisenman), such a partitioning would seem to offer little to the present debate. Nonetheless, differing attitudes toward these techniques reveal a telling shift in the conceptual and material ambitions of the younger generation from those of Eisenman's own.

Lacking the opportunities to pursue much built work in the economically depressed 1970s, many architects of Eisenman's generation turned their attention to theoretical projects and so-called "paper architecture." Much has been made of the conceptual significance of these works, but there has been surprisingly little mention of the objects themselves – the elegant drawings, models, and collages that these investigations produced.[4] Eisenman's cold, ink-on-mylar axonometrics that appear in *Terragni* and illustrate his early houses, as well as the work of many of his contemporaries, exhibit a clinical, machinic rigor that belies the fact that each is an exquisitely handcrafted object. For all their foregrounding of abstract intellection, latent in these works (and decidedly absent from the few built projects of the period) is a highly sophisticated attention to craft and detail and their consequent tactile and material effects.

Today, all but a few retrograde practitioners have abandoned such painstaking analog processes for the relative immediacy of the digital. Some designers (including Eisenman) now employ the possibilities of the computer as a means of advancing this project of abstract formal investigation. For others, the ability of digital processes to precisely depict the material effects suppressed by Eisenman in his built work has led to the abandonment of abstract form in favor of the visceral articulation of environments.

Of course, Eisenman's use of the terms *analog* and *digital* implies much more than a degree of allegiance to computer-based design processes. He described analog projects as indices of abstract information in physical form, by definition intimately tied to problems of legibility and meaning. Such indexical operations have been crucial to Eisenman's work throughout his career, both as a means to manipulate abstract form as well as to embed referential information within those forms. Digital projects, on the other hand, simply employ certain computational techniques with no clear relation to meaning or history. Clearly uncomfortable with such independence of form and content, Eisenman questioned the possibility of judgment and disciplinary identity in the absence of legibility.[5] For Eisenman, the real danger is not that digital processes will displace analog ones, but rather that in the use of digital processes, architecture may very well displace its own history.

5. Eisenman even questioned this lack of legibility in his own work, claiming that without the clear process of his earlier projects, he "did not know how to make the form" of the Naples proposal.

Of the five presenters, Greg Lynn most directly extends the formal investigations of Peter Eisenman. Charting a course from work he began in Eisenman's office (especially on the Frankfurt Biocentrum project and Aronoff Center for Design and Art in Cincinnati), Lynn demonstrated how his own work turns away from Eisenman's simple primitive forms (grids, cubes, bars, and L-forms) and geometrical transformations (rotations, scalings, doublings, etc.), in favor of calculus-based operations on complex primitives such as spline surfaces and blob (isometric polysurface) forms. Suggesting that Frankfurt and Cincinnati were "analog projects that wanted to be digital," Lynn portrayed his own work as the natural progression of Eisenman's formal manipulations into the digital age.

Wes Jones, who spent his time in Eisenman's office working on the more semantically driven Wexner Center for the Arts, labors in his own projects to "soup up" the representational effects of architectural form. Transforming architectural precedents ranging from Le Corbusier's chaise lounge to ordinary shipping containers, Jones employs this hot rod analogy as a means to manipulate legible forms toward what he termed MAYA - the "most advanced yet acceptable" level. As such, Jones aspires to test but not transgress the perceived limits of the discipline.

In diverse projects such as a health spa in the Okavango delta in Botswana, a bar in New York's meatpacking district, a store outfitted for Issey Miyake, and an extreme skiing outpost in Alaska, Lindy Roy redirects Eisenman's formal manipulations to perpetrate elegant visual and tactile effects with materially specific elements such as fiber optic strands,

FREE! MUSCLE COURSE THAT CAN ADD 3 INCHES TO YOUR ARMS FAST!
...AND BUILD YOU INTO A NEW FORM MAKER!!!

In half the time, with twice the ease, in the privacy of your own room, in just a few minutes a day, I will, through my TRIPLE PROGRESSION COURSE, that I want to send you FREE, guarantee that virtually overnight, you will experience a muscle-building miracle! Before your eyes you will slap on inches of steel-hard muscles to your pipe-stem arms, pack your chest with power and size, give yourself life-guard shoulders and dynamic, speedy, athletic legs. Add jet-charged strength to every muscle! I do not care if, today, you own the scraggiest, flabbiest, skinniest, or funniest-looking body, whether you are tall or short, young or not-so-young,

skinny or fat, office worker, laborer, Knowlton School student or perhaps a businessperson. I must make a new, supercharged form maker out of you— with handsome muscles bursting out all over! They will ripple with power, vibrate with energy! What I did for Greg Lynn, 2001 Mr. Universe winner, and hundreds of other champions since 1990, I am ready to do for you! A-C-T-I-O-N is the key for strength! Fill out the coupon below now! Rush it to me- and in hours, at no charge to you- at my own expense, you too, like Greg Lynn did, will start putting an end to your weakness! ACT NOW! SUPPLY IS LIMITED!

THIS GIANT 32 PAGE COURSE *ABSOLUTELY FREE!*

WRITE TO: JEFFREY KIPNIS Dept. 83-11C
TRAINER OF CHAMPIONS SINCE 1990.
190 WEST SEVENTEENTH AVENUE, COLUMBUS 43210

Dear Jeff: Shoot the Works! I am saying YES to becoming a New Designer! Rush me your Free Muscle-Building information which I can use right now at my academic or practice-oriented institution to build handsome and useful additions to all discourses of shape making.

I enclose only $3.99 to cover the cost of handling and mailing. I am under no further obligation.

NAME: ---
ADDRESS: --
CITY: ----------------------------------- STATE: -------
ZIP CODE: ------------------------------ AGE: ----
(Please print clearly)

translucent glass and plastic, and, at her Subwave installation at P. S. 1, even mist. Though her operational strategies are similar to Eisenman's, Roy shifts attention away from the forms themselves toward their resultant atmospheric effects.[6]

Like Roy, Thomas Leeser works to engage visitors directly with visual effects. Where Eisenman utilizes outside information to manipulate form, Leeser indexes his projects' programs to articulate surface. Using digital technologies, Leeser inscribes his projects with ephemeral traces of program, creating vital environments that constantly change according to the actions of their occupants. Footsteps are temporarily recorded on digital floors, web use is translated onto the wall surfaces of an internet company, and dynamic structural loading is mapped onto the truss work of a bridge through complex sensors linked to color-coded lighting. Often deployed within generic interiors, Leeser's projects constituted the conference's least formally exuberant but most legibly indexical designs.

In projects such as the Torus House and the Tel Aviv Museum of Art, Preston Scott Cohen, drawing upon extensive research of projective geometry and stereotomy, exhibits

6. To generate the seductive forms of her projects, Roy indexes such diverse processes as Vidal Sassoon hair cutting techniques, theoretical biology, and the formation of termite mounds.

a predilection for formal manipulations akin to Greg Lynn's, though his interests lie not in the logic of complex surfaces but rather in the volumetric possibilities of traditional architectural space-making. Cohen, like Eisenman, has also devoted considerable attention to the Italian baroque.[7] For Eisenman, these investigations serve as catalysts to foster a close reading of the architectural object. By contrast, Cohen deploys the lessons of the baroque to generate atmospheric effects best experienced through distracted attention.[8]

Though the above descriptions suggest a partitioning of the participants, with Lynn, Cohen, and Jones as sympathetic to Eisenman's formal ambitions and Roy and Leeser setting out to contrast them, such an assessment would be disingenuous. In spite of their superficial differences, and regardless of the undeniable strength of their respective investigations, each participant ultimately represents a predictable trajectory from Eisenman himself. Whether form is agitated according to complex computational procedures (Lynn, Cohen), semantic information (Jones, Leeser), or both (Roy), the primary mechanism of each of these practices, as with Eisenman's own, is the index – the instrumentalization of information to manipulate form and generate effects.[9] As such, each participant leaves Eisenman's fundamental position on the primacy of formal manipulation, legibility, and indexicality effectively unchallenged.

In leaving Eisenman's intellectual project of indexicality intact, each protégé failed to deploy Eisenman's most potent technique – criticality. In his keynote address, Eisenman presented the history of architecture as serial patricide – each generation perpetrating critical displacements on what has come before. This genealogical model affords any discipline its specific history and maintains its autonomy from other cultural practices. But over the last thirty years, the so-called "critical project" has become not only more pervasive but also increasingly internalized and self-referential, transforming a revolutionary ethos into a formulaic technique. The resulting predictability elicits a perverse oxymoron: the status quo of the avant-garde. Or, in the words of Reyner Banham, "New shapes notwithstanding, it is still the same old architecture, in the sense that the architects involved have relied on their inherited sense of primacy in the building team, and have insisted that they alone shall determine the forms to be employed. Formalism it may be, but it remains formalism within the limits of a professional tradition."[10]

Banham's quip comes from his two-part essay "Stocktaking," of 1960, in which he railed against such narrow

7. As the only presenter never to have been employed in Eisenman's office, Cohen's relationship to Eisenman's historical teachings (and his difference from the other presenters) might be attributed to his having been Eisenman's student at Harvard.

8. For more on Cohen's relationship to the baroque and his production of atmospheric effects, see Sylvia Lavin, "The Three Faces of Tel Aviv," Tel Aviv Museum of Art exhibition catalogue. See also Cohen's own *Contested Symmetries and other Predicaments in Architecture* (New York: Princeton Architectural Press, 2001).

9. Stan Allen describes the index as "a series of clues pointing back to the event of design and the hand of the author. This is a fundamentally modern practice, reflecting a belief in the object's capacity to carry traces of its origin and making a corresponding belief in interpretation as unmasking a self-referential play of meaning." See his "Tracks, Traces, Tricks," in *ANY* 0 (May/June 1993): 10. See also Rosalind Krauss, "Notes on the Index," *October* 3 and 4 (1977), a text Eisenman cited in his keynote address as influential for his own understanding of the term.

10. Reyner Banham, "Stocktaking" *Architectural Review* 127 (February 1960). Reprinted in *A Critic Writes: Essay by Reyner Banham,* ed. Mary. Banham et al.(Berkeley: University of California Press, 1996,: 54.

11. Ibid., 61.

views of the profession. Under the heading "Tradition," he placed those who espoused the "operational lore" of architecture, the set of techniques and habits that architects have maintained and passed down through generations of masters and pupils. Emphasis is placed on history, disciplinary autonomy, and the formal and representational properties of the objects produced. In contrast, Banham proposed "Technology," a faction made up in large part of nonarchitects and specialists "ignorant of the lore of the operation," a group capable of "creat[ing] an Other Architecture by chance, as it were, out of apparent intelligence and the task of creating fit environments for human activities."[11]

Exchanging Banham's Tradition/Technology with contemporary terms – difficult/easy, critical/projective, indexical/diagrammatic, life/lifestyle – provides a fair assessment of the state of current debate.[12] As one camp circles the wagons in order to fend off onslaughts against architecture's autonomy, the other welcomes all comers to the party.

Alone among the participants at the conference, R. E. Somol has aligned himself with the latter group. Celebrating the possibilities of a more expansive field he writes: "One aspect of this reorientation would be to recognize (and possibly profit from) architecture's erosion by surrounding design fields, the slackening of the discipline, its dissolution into graphic, landscape, product, interior, fashion, and urban 'design.' All design fields are in the process of becoming-one. What's becoming 'out of place' is the role of disciplinarity in the communion of information technology and the virtuality of materials."[13]

A broader sampling of Eisenman's progeny could possibly have provoked such a debate. Architects such as Mark Wamble of Interloop Architects and Sarah Whiting of WW both spent time in Eisenman's office before setting off in directions remarkably different from the indexical investigations seen here. But in a cunning act of synecdoche, "The Shape of Things to Come" presented a single facet of the discipline as the whole of architectural culture, and in so doing severely limited the possibilities of the conference.

12. For a historical perspective, Marshall McLuhan's terms hot/cool (invoked at this conference by R.E. Somol), form/function, and even *Moderne/Ancien* may be added to the list.
13. R.E. Somol, "In the Wake of *Assemblage*," *Assemblage* 41 (2000): 93.

TODD GANNON TEACHES AT THE KNOWLTON SCHOOL OF ARCHITECTURE AT OHIO STATE, WHERE HE EDITS THE SERIES *SOURCE BOOKS IN ARCHITECTURE*, WHICH INCLUDES *UN STUDIO/ERASMUS BRIDGE*, *BERNARD TSCHUMI/ZÉNITH DE ROUEN*, *MORPHOSIS/DIAMOND RANCH HIGH SCHOOL*, AND *THE LIGHT CONSTRUCTION READER*.

PROGRESS ON THE SEINE RIVE
GAUCHE PROJECT IN THE 13TH
ARRONDISEMENT OF PARIS. SEEN
HERE ARE THE AUSTERLITZ AND
TOLBIAC DISTRICTS AS OF JANUARY
2004. PHOTOS: SAM WOODWORTH.

*Not far from the serene garden that Dominique Perrault has sunk
between the towers of France's new National Library, heavy
machinery is inscribing the latest phase of Seine Rive Gauche upon
300 acres of eastern Paris. Some contend that the crowd of planners
and architects at work here took a few too many cues from
Haussmann, but even where uncompleted city blocks bleed into
expanses of mud, there is a remarkably rich variety of textures
interwoven through a topographical sensitivity that is hardly
Haussmannian. At the unpretentious crossing of Voies EC/13 and
EE/13 – provisional street names oddly featured in classic Parisian
signage – there unfolds a panorama of mills and silos. This is the
patrimoine industriel whose handing under the project prompted
outcry among artists and others occupying the buildings until
recently. Markers of the industrial past, these structures will be
preserved, but no less enveloped by a project whose inaugural rai-
son d'être in 1985 was to infuse the soured economy of eastern
Paris with a tertiary flavor. Yet in its diverse programming, rhythmic massing sequence, and whimsical details, Seine Rive Gauche
renounces the icy urban modernism of La Défense and the equally
frigid postmodernism of New York's Battery Park City. Here is a
permeable and heterogeneous space, animated by forces scholarly,
commercial, domestic, and religious. After all, who needed another
Canary Wharf?* – Sam Woodworth

Luis Fernández-Galiano

The Butterfly's Fate: In Praise of Oxymoron

–I am glad it's over. This joint venture between Rem Koolhaas and Jacques Herzog was doomed from the beginning.

–You mean to say you were hoping it would fail. Mixing fire and water never appealed to you.

–On the contrary! Rem thought that many were waiting to be disappointed, but some of us simply doubted a ship could sail with two captains. Architecture may be a choral business, and we may be sick and tired of the signature thing, but, at the end of the day, a project needs someone in charge. Of course, there is this utopian strand, from Tatlin's collective artist to the Rockefeller's design by committee, that tries to dissolve authorship, and look where it has taken us: bureaucratic town planning and corporate architecture. Do you think design by committee is going to produce a new Rockefeller Center at Ground Zero?

–Here you are being unfair. Daniel Libeskind and David Childs' cohabitation does not exactly resemble a romance, and in any case SOM has been put at the helm, so your concern for every enterprise having a CEO would be met here. As you know only too well, the collaboration between OMA and H&deM was sparked by mutual admiration, so theirs was no arranged marriage of convenience. And the fact that the two firms were the most influential of recent years made their coming together even more exciting. I only miss a good picture of Rem and Jacques that could stay down for the record, like the one taken of Le Corbusier and Mies at the Weissenhof!

–The missing photo-op is probably a good reminder that the Weissenhof happened, whereas Astor Place didn't. In Stuttgart, Mies was in charge of the Siedlung, and of course both he and Corbu carried out their buildings independently. But who was Ian Schrager supposed to phone up to discuss details? Kissinger once complained that he didn't know Europe's phone number, and perhaps the developer of Astor Place didn't know the numbers of his European architects either. When he got fed up and tried to clear the ground, Jacques was elegant enough to decline the offer, so the commission ended up in the predictable hands of Frank Gehry – a serial killer who is still waiting for a Manhattan victim!

–But this is certainly not the case with Prada. There,

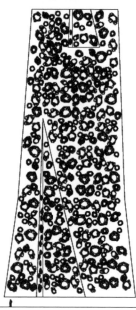

Herzog & de Meuron in collaboration with Rem Koolhaas, studies for the Astor Place Hotel, New York. Model courtesy OMA, sketch courtesy Herzog & de Meuron.

Patrizio Bertelli knew well whom to call for the New York store, and whom for Tokyo's.

—Which is the reason the Prada jobs were completed. OMA in Soho and H&deM in Omotesando had a rather straightforward brief: sexing up a fashion brand with trophy architecture. Forget about Koolhaas trying to reinvent shopping or Herzog counterpoising with a store is a store is a store. In the end, they both produced fine works, overflowing with intellectual sophistication and visual refinement, even if for a sadly trivial purpose. But was this a collaboration proper? Working for the same client, like building on nearby sites in the same scheme, may account for closer contact, more intimate dialogue, and stronger mutual influence, but it's nothing like painting on the same canvas.

—You know, Deyan Sudjic has described Jacques and Rem as the Picasso and Braque of contemporary architecture, roped together like mountaineers climbing to the summit, and I feel he's on to something. I am aware they are not playing four-hands piano: their output has been so consistently diverse that the joint-invention-of-cubism metaphor is somehow off the mark. But in their ground-breaking ambition and close attention to each other there is a scent of the Picasso-Braque story.

—And yet please note that even in such a carefully honed artistic partnership, each painter produced his own works! Picasso and Matisse, always keeping an eye toward and trying to learn from each other, might have perhaps supplied a better comparison, and one that would account for the competitive factor. When the Schrager commission was being developed, with all those teams going back and forth between Rotterdam and Basel, I never had the feeling of a jam session, with the musicians effortlessly weaving a tune, but rather of watching one of those Colombian accordion contests in which two players start with different rhythms and each struggles to bring the rival into his own melody.

—These were not the intentions behind the collaboration at Astor Place. Rem has explained how it arose out of frustration with the waste of a competition system that pits architects against one another, and out of fatigue with the insistent demand of a characteristic style from each. Of course, the move also claimed to explore strategic alliances in a globalized world, but this is the kind of management lingo he uses to place his projects in the XL sphere of political economy. Deep down, I believe working together was about learning, friendship, and fun. Rem had suggested to Jacques doing the Tate together back in 1994, and five years later the

GRAPHIC DIAGRAM OF THE ASTOR PLACE HOTEL. IMAGE COURTESY HERZOG & DE MEURON.

Schrager hotel offered a second window of opportunity – this time leading to more than 18 months of close cooperation, abruptly ended by the client.

–So maybe Ian Schrager is the one to blame here. I remember the last revision of the project, undertaken at his demand, that transformed the haphazard pattern of holes of the outer envelope into camouflaged, irregular windows, thereby giving a clue as to scale and draining all the energy from the shape. But it appears that even this watered-down version was too risqué for him. Or perhaps Rem antagonized him with his dour attitude and brisk manners, who knows. In any case, it seems more than clear that you need a good client to get good results. Miuccia Prada has indeed been very different, and who would not prefer working with her *concetto* than with Donatella Versace's? Although very often I wonder why all these haute couture clients have become obligatory reference for the finest talents in the profession?

–Don't start moralizing now. You're probably right in describing Astor Place as an impossible job, lacking as it did a clear leadership. But the experience was refreshingly innovative, brazenly political, and more than generous. And where do you find clients for this sort of laboratory but in the upper tier of the luxury market for merchandise or leisure? Prada, Schrager, Guggenheim . . . Commerce as culture or culture as commerce, who cares? When boundaries blur, those on the border are better placed to shape the future. So don't lecture us on the frivolous nature of fashion architecture.

OMA, Prada Epicenter, New York. Photo: Armin Linke.

–All right, *touché*. Now, be frank. Did you really buy Rem's enthusiasm about shopping, or his interest in fashion as a pure form of recreation that opens the door to the sublime? Weren't you disappointed by the Prada book, more an overblown PR handout than the self-aware volume one expects from an accomplished writer and brilliant designer? Aren't you rather fed up with all this press coverage of Kool Rem as a fashion guru, the ultimate expert on the brand value of celebrity architecture? Because – full disclosure – I couldn't stand seeing the author of *Delirious New York* and *S, M, L, XL* sequestered by the junk world of advertising copy as a merchandising tie-in of a season campaign, only to end up featured in the money shot of a gangbang!

–Come on, hold it. Don't get carried away. How do you know he was not a helpless fashion victim but, as some customers describe themselves, a happy victim of fashion? As a consultant of Condé Nast, he has had more than enough opportunities to realize that there is no real difference between custom magazines and custom architecture, and as an author of Taschen, he is in the core of a publishing mutation which is morphing art from middlebrow to cool, taking pornography from brown envelopes to K-Mart, and bringing design from cult books to coffee tables. The last Koolhaas may be Rem lite, but he is certainly a voluntary prisoner of the ¥€$ world of global logos and no-friction capital.

–I hope you are aware of the irony of describing Koolhaas, the most abrasive of architects, happily drifting in the no-friction amniotic fluid of global fashion! At any rate, I am willing to admit that fashion is an interest he shares with Herzog, although with a rather different approach. In contrast with Rem's sociological – or even geopolitical – vision,

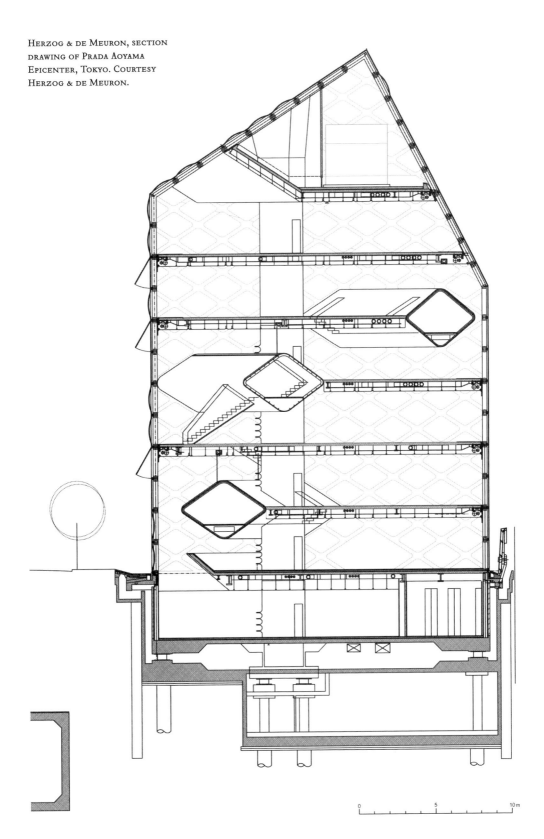

HERZOG & DE MEURON, SECTION
DRAWING OF PRADA AOYAMA
EPICENTER, TOKYO. COURTESY
HERZOG & DE MEURON.

0   5   10m

Jacques' perception is softer, subtler, closer to art proper and the textile as the ur-material of enclosure and protection – the Beuys-Semper connection. But if I was reluctant to see them working together, it was not because they were doing it in a fashion-leisure context. Granted, after 9/11, wishful thinking projected a blackout of the frivolous, and we are all in a shifting intellectual ground that tinges the nineties retrospectively. However, my main contention with the OMA-H&deM collaboration was aesthetic, and dealt with authorship. In the same way I cannot imagine Picasso and Matisse touching the same canvas, I simply cannot picture Koolhaas and Herzog in concert!

–Something which is clearly contradicted by the many successful partnerships in the history of architecture. Herzog & de Meuron, to begin with, is a good example of this shared approach to design, and one that can develop into a collective endeavor, as Jacques and Pierre have proven with the extension of professional and artistic responsibility to Harry Gugger and Christine Binswanger. I fear you understood this joint venture, or strategic alliance, as rather a friendly take-over bid to line up Jacques with Bruce Mau, Cecil Balmond, or Sanford Kwinter in Rem's galaxy.

–Well, you see, companies may grow organically with new partners, or merge fusing their corporate cultures, but they cannot survive without leadership, and pretty much the same thing has always happened in the art world. Titian or Rubens, for instance, had large ateliers, but it was finally the master who took care of the more critical commissions, or the one who painted faces and hands, leaving drapery or landscapes to assistants. Even if understanding OMA and H&deM as no more than design firms, how do you bring together such different creatures? OMA is a top-heavy company, greatly geared to Rem's mood, perpetually reinventing itself, entering the Royal Haskoning Group or growing branches like AMO, swift-moving and unpredictable. H&deM is the product of gradual growth, extremely cautious, conservative, and reliable in the Swiss tradition, slow-changing and very competently run. Shortly after starting to work together, Rem already felt they were partners, while for Jacques they were simply collaborating in a small commission. The perceptions were different, and both avoided the real issue – who is leading the art team?

—It seems you think it impossible to have two heavy-weights in the same boat.

–I think it's impossible to have two at the helm! Art, in the end, is a very solitary business. Collaboration is a term that stands for subordination or specialization more often than for dialogue. Some have suggested that OMA and H&deM could be complementary, with OMA at the XL scale of regional planning and H&deM at the XS end of building detail, thereby merging the territorial and the tactile, but of course Koolhaas is also an extraordinary designer of small works and Herzog & de Meuron have produced several significant urban plans, so I am afraid we cannot get off the hook that way.

–You still have one path to explore, although perhaps one that wouldn't make Jacques entirely happy. Following Rem's attachment to surrealism, you could present this ephemeral alliance – and indeed any artistic partnership – as a *cadavre exquis,* after the game in which Breton and his friends wrote poetry by adding words without knowing the preceding one.

–An exquisite corpse indeed, and a game in the end: *that* could be a good description of this collaboration! Koolhaas has used the method frequently in his own work, but the process demands slicing up the commission and designing the parts independently, something which wasn't easy at Astor Place, where you could only clearly segregate core and crust – a more organic way of approaching it, and one that would lead towards an inevitably specialized assignation of roles.

–All right, I accept that the difficulties of working together in the Manhattan hotel were perhaps too many to grant an uneventful sail, but I think the challenge was precisely there. And would you deny that rubbing shoulders has made Koolhaas more materially aware and Herzog more graphically eloquent? Haven't they learned from each other? Haven't they moved closer? Look at the Beijing projects, the CCTV tower and the stadium, through which Rem and Jacques are going to provide the built symbols of the 2008 Olympic Games. Beside the obvious traces of intervention by the engineer Cecil Balmond, who has worked with both of them in these Chinese commissions, one can perceive a rather visible convergence, which may be due to the very nature of the work – logo buildings for a world event – but that may also stem from this long period of frequent contact.

–Beijing is indeed the proof of the cake, because there Koolhaas and Herzog are going to perform on the same stage – and a huge one at that! However closer their approaches have moved, Beijing is about emulation and competition. Of course, the convenient and slightly lazy confrontation between the artificially modern Dutch and the naturally archaic Swiss will be more than blurred by distance and scale, but loop and nest will remain as shorthand, ready-to-use metaphors for these neatly different interpretations of togetherness.

−So you feel there is still some truth in the common critical depiction of Koolhaas and Herzog as opposed poles of contemporary architecture.

−Some indeed, although of course less than before. I never straightjacketed them into the diminishing labels of journalist or cosmetician, however much I admired the muscular writings of Koolhaas or the refined skins of Herzog. But I have often used the rhetorical opposition between the two as a pedagogical tool to describe the current landscape. Somehow, Rem and Jacques were the perfect representation of Vico's split between the intellect, dealing with truth, and the imagination, which belongs to the realm of poetic expression. Words versus images, but also life versus art, in a very fitting illustration of that early aesthetic divide between the effort to come to terms with the world and the will to create a world-in-itself, that artistic microcosm that Baumgarten would call "heterocosm." If you allow me the pedantry, I would add that Koolhaas's path is the one charted in Aristotle's *Poetics,* while Herzog's follows more closely that advocated in Plato's *Republic.*

−The last thing I would expect is a case for an Aristotelian Rem and a Platonic Jacques! Realism versus idealism, or narrativity versus aestheticism should be more than enough to describe the quite obvious tension between understanding and pleasure that distinguishes their respective attitudes. As far as I can tell, Rem's literary rationalism makes him something of an honorary Frenchman, surrealist strand included, while Jacques's visual romanticism is firmly rooted in his Germanic humus, so their dialogue would seem to extend a time-honored conversation.

−The conversation between the intellectual and the artist? Or the conversation between the moralist who thinks that art imitates life and the formalist who claims that, on the contrary, life imitates art?

−Well, Jacques as a formalist I can still make out. But are you calling Rem a moralist? The man conventionally presented as the archetypal cynical architect, a moralist?

−A neorealist, a social realist, a moralist, call him what you will. Or even a cynic in the Greek sense of the word. Think twice and you will see that this is not as outrageous as it seems. But what really interests me in the affair is that joining Rem and Jacques begets a philosophical monster and an artistic oxymoron. As an intellectual centaur or mermaid, it is an untenable chimera. But as an architectural oxymoron, it is an unstable relationship that, however brief the bond, splits releasing energy and changing the trajectory of both elementary particles. Rem has described both of them feeling trapped in their assigned stylistic spaces, pinned by needles on a board like butterflies, and how collaborating was a way of getting rid of those fixed identities. If one simply considers the fate of Astor Place, most would write it off in the debt column. But if you pull in the dazzling weight of the Beijing projects and their vanishing identity, one cannot but bow in praise of architectural oxymoron.

–Perhaps our only hope of avoiding the butterfly's fate!

LUIS FERNÁNDEZ-GALIANO IS THE ARCHITECTURE CRITIC OF *EL PAIS* AND EDITOR OF *ARQUITECTURA VIVA* IN MADRID. "THE BUTTERFLY'S FATE" ALSO APPEARS IN *CONTENT*, PUBLISHED ON THE OCCASION OF THE OMA EXHIBITION AT THE NATIONAL GALLERY IN BERLIN IN FALL 2003.

Looks like working with Prada has launched Rem Koolhaas and
OMA into a whole new line: T-shirts. Not just any old T-shirts,
but "exclusive OMA–AMO T-shirts" emblazoned, to greater and
lesser graphic success, with various OMA architectural and graphic
productions. This Mao-red chemise of course features the already
iconic CCTV Tower awaiting construction in Beijing. Our lender of
said T immediately refashioned it, cutting into the neckline to make
the rude garment more fetching. (OMA, are you listening?) The
shirts were sold at the National Gallery in Berlin during the OMA
exhibition "Content" and, according to the exhibition "catalogue"
of the same name, were also available on e-bay from Christmas
Eve to New Year's Eve. Also available were white muscle-T's
featuring "when buildings attack," sinister-looking cartoons of
silhouetted OMA buildings made human. But perhaps the most
sinister of all was the fuscia-on-white Whitney Museum scheme
labeled "NO!" – The Log Team

Sarah Whiting

Thick Thin

Weighed down by a simultaneous envy and fear of the ephemeral, architects are once again trying to push _beinahe_ ever closer to _nichts_: triple glazing has attained single-paned depths; transparency and translucency are _de rigueur_; structure is at once lighter and stronger. This contemporary minimalism strives for entry to an architectural El Dorado suspended between the here and the after – a diaphanous present that carries no weight. SANAA's Park Café in Koga (1996-1998) or their Day Care Center for the Elders in Yokohama (1997-2000) immediately come to mind. Both projects gracefully slip into their contexts, the first becoming the natural surroundings of a provincial park, the second the dense urbanism of Yokohama. SANAA's minimalism is astonishingly beautiful. Exploiting contemporary techniques, their buildings are more about surface and detailing than Miesian proportion and materiality. Albeit beautiful when done well – which is all too rare, given the demands it makes on construction – minimalism as an aspiration risks propagating architectural banality: by standing so still, so quietly, so _barely there_, such projects can all too often tumble into nothingness.

Rather than stilling and silencing, Rem Koolhaas and the Office for Metropolitan Architecture's recently completed McCormick Campus Center at the Illinois Institute of Technology (IIT) in Chicago transforms and amplifies at every turn. Here the material thinness of minimalism is replaced by an architecture of fattened flatness. The center's thick thinness goes beyond Mies not by aspiring to his almost-nothingness but by multiplying _somethingness_. Chicago is flat. And nothing is more Chicago than IIT. But at the McCormick Center, flat is thick. A building that is all about plan is knowable only as section. Its single story holds together many levels, including a suspended – or is it dropped? – garden of grasses above the food court. The theme of this split-screen vision of nature-prairie and culture-cafeteria continues one bay north from the cafeteria, where Mies's original Commons lies preserved. The earth around the Commons has been excavated, making the building like an artifact from Pompeian ruins that Koolhaas claimed as the project's organizational inspiration. The revealed base of the Commons has been

Scenes from an October afternoon at the McCormick Campus
Center. Row 1: approaching from
the south; row 2: approaching
from the west; row 3: graphic
thick thinness; rows 4 & 5: horizontal and vertical transparency.
Photos: Sarah Whiting.

Koolhaas meets Mies: Rows 1–3: intersections and adjacencies of two buildings; rows 4 &5: internal landscaping and the tube that internalizes, however briefly, the Chicago elevated trains. Photos: Sarah Whiting.

painted a deep matte black, turning it into a heavy pedestal for this unburied archaeological treasure. Sectional depth is further accentuated by transverse experience: here, the axial is replaced by the diagonal, which means that everything is viewed on the oblique, offering depth of field rather than the singularity of the axial one-point perspective.

But the McCormick Center's vertical surfaces are what bring the greatest depth to thinness. Like the work of Herzog & de Meuron and Neutelings/Riedijk, straight up is where the building offers a direct challenge to the minimalist tendency toward immateriality. But while those two firms emphasize pattern and image, the façades of OMA's McCormick Center rely more upon thickness than surface. Glass here sheds aspirations to nondimensional transparency or two-dimensional imagery: honeycombed Panelite is embedded within a double-glazed system, making air itself substantial. When the afternoon sun hits the orange Panelite of the zigzagging primary façade, the spaces behind it become a single, massive orange swath, an interiorized sunset fog. As night falls, loopy orange halos appear and disappear, headlights passing down State Street wreaking circular havoc within this faceted orthogonal façade.

Why orange? Koolhaas asserts that its extreme contrast to the surrounding black and tan Mies buildings helps bring out their subtle colors – which is true. But orange offers more than an accent. The British publication *Business Week* calls orange the new corporate color, chosen for its seeming combination of the cutting edge and innocence, a fitting description for Koolhaas's practice as it negotiates between the avant garde and consumption.[1] Orange, which happens to be the national color of the Netherlands (is OMA deliberately putting a Dutch stamp on a German icon in the U.S.?), is also the hue of low caffeine and high fat. Sanka forever cast orange as the color of decaf, and, banking on psychologists' claims that orange is an appetite stimulant, fast food chains have long saturated their restaurants in its various hues. So what's the message of this medium? There isn't *one* – orange keeps appearing in a different light, as it were. Architecture's singular message is what is being called into question; the decorated shed no longer has one sign but many.

Strangely, this saturation does not result in chaos. The verticals of the McCormick Center fade in and fade out, accumulating without competing. The lenticular wallpapers (squiggly brown and tan stripes in the faculty dining room; orange – again – and black squiggles in the meeting rooms) make the flat walls almost fuzzy. The graphic mastery of

1. See Lynn Shepherd, "Any Colour You Like, As Long as it's Orange," *Business Life* (July/August 2003): 36-40. Also see Sylvia Lavin's recent research on color, "Color, Terminable and Interminable," lecture, Harvard GSD, October 28, 2003.

REM KOOLHAAS AND PHYLLIS
LAMBERT TOUR THE CENTER.
PHOTO: SARAH WHITING.

2x4's Michael Rock truly transforms the wall-as-sign. Rock designed what seem to be hundreds of two-and-a-half-inch-high black-and-white icons, new "universal" figures denoting tasks like computing, sleeping, music, and even romance (abstracted as a flower held in the teeth of a standing figure). Crowded together on panels, these figures collect to form larger icons, in a kind of pixilated pointillism. On one long wall their dot matrix offers an IIT history lesson by illustrating the institution's founding fathers (Armour, Heald, Pritzker, Galvin, and a young Mies) in a 21st-century version of the obligatory Ivy League gallery of portraits. But the most clever, most unsettling portrait is that of the fully mature, slightly dour Mies, whose head, split horizontally into an orange/white top and clear/white bottom, constitutes the building's front door. It's *Being John Malkovitch* (who is from Chicago, after all) merged with Samuel Beckett's *The Unnammable*:

Perhaps that's what I feel, an outside and an inside and me in the middle, perhaps that's what I am, the thing that divides the world in two, on the one side the outside, on the other the inside, that can be as thin as foil, I'm neither one side nor the other, I'm in the middle, I'm the partition, I've two surfaces and no thickness, perhaps that's what I feel, myself vibrating, I'm the tympanum, on the one hand the mind, on the other the world, I don't belong to either . . . [2]

2. Samuel Beckett, *Three Novels: Malloy, Malone Dies, The Unnamable* (New York: Grove Press, 1958), 383.

Irreverent? Yes, maybe, although a 16-foot-high portrait facing a major thoroughfare is also an honor to which no other architect can lay claim. It's Mies, translated through the technology institute's dot-matrix dialect; it's Mies, reminding everyone of his everlasting importance at IIT; it's Mies, trapped in the vibrations of the ever-multiplying interpretations of himself and his oeuvre. But mostly, it's the students, the many tympanums suspended in the center between classes – and between childhood and adulthood. The multiplicities, simultaneities, and densities of the McCormick Center's thickened thinness capture this uncertainty and turn it into possibility, animation, and information rather than chaos, disorientation and estrangement. Thick Thin! Thick Different!

SARAH WHITING IS ASSOCIATE
PROFESSOR OF ARCHITECTURE AT
HARVARD'S GRADUATE SCHOOL OF
DESIGN, AND A PARTNER IN THE
ARCHITECTURAL FIRM WW IN
SOMERVILLE, MASSACHUSETTS.

Phyllis Lambert

Love in the Time
Of the WTC

How far are we from Thomas Alva Edison's claim that every American baby cranes its neck in its cradle to see how it can build a better one? The quest for a better cradle ran the historical gamut of architectural approaches in recent proposals for the rebuilding of the World Trade Center (WTC) site – from mimesis and archaeology to baroque effulgence, *architecture parlante*, and contemporary philosophy. Ultimately, however, the impulse to build a "better cradle" early in the 21st century too often bows to the pragmatics of a marketplace Edison would barely recognize.

What is sadly absent in the dominance of the marketplace – in the time of the WTC – is the love of architecture. There are heady expressions of love found throughout the historical literature on architecture – in Alberti's *De re aedificatoria*, in Filarete's *Trattato* ("building is nothing more than a voluptuous pleasure"), and in Francesco Colonna's *Hypnerotomachia Poliphilo*.[1] This love begins not necessarily with the architect but with ownership – what it means to be a patron or client – and even more, with responsible *stewardship*. Commissioning and building "ambitious" architecture is one thing; caring for it, loving it, is yet another. Once great architecture has been commissioned, once a patron has ensured that it is built in a way that gives concrete form to the significance of the architectural idea, to what extent can a building's fate be guaranteed against the unknowable and uncontrollable future?

In the 20th century, two projects stand out as canonic examples of the love of architecture: Mies van der Rohe's paradigmatic Farnsworth House and Seagram Building. Both embody his typologies of choice: the clear-span and the high-rise. In these two striking cases, which marked a new high in American architecture – a moment in the 1950s when North American architecture responded equally to industrial and spiritual imperatives – Mies worked closely with committed patrons, Dr. Edith Farnsworth and the Seagram Company, whose love of architecture was played out in surprisingly different ways, but both of whom eventually ceded ownership of the buildings they commissioned, leaving them to the vicissitudes of human fortune.

1. Alberti reflected on how a beautiful building fulfills the architect's passion for building as much as it satisfies the patron's desire to appreciate and praise powerful works. Filarete likened the conception of a building to the way a man and woman together bring a child into being. Colonna's *Hyperotomachia Phliphilo*, or strife of love in a dream, opens up beyond *mathemata*, proportion, and aesthetic value. It unfolds further in the erotic impulse to articulate – as Alberto Pérez Gómez reminds us in his *Polyphilo, or, The Dark Forest Revisited* (1992) – the existential condition to which humanity can only be reconciled within the culture of art and architecture and the metaphoric imagination.

31

From the outset, Mies's two clients were motivated by very different desires: Dr. Farnsworth's romantic devotion to the person of the architect, and Seagram's commitment to build in the best possible way for its time, to realize Mies's architectural idea to its fullest, and to create a new kind of public space for New York. This can be traced through the histories of each building. Indeed, the ownership histories of Farnsworth and Seagram resemble the pathway Dante constructed in his *Divine Comedy,* in which the seven deadly sins of earthly love (or lust), pride, avarice, envy, wrath, gluttony, and sloth move between Hell and Paradise, opposed by the virtues of Platonic love, modesty or humility, generosity, kindness, restraint or self-control, faith and temperance, and zeal.

Dr. Farnsworth struggled between the inner and outer natures of an art, and ultimately was unable to devote herself equally to both. She created a rift where there should have been a growing understanding of Mies's vision, not to mention her distortion of the architect-client relationship. The forces of lustful love blinded her to Mies's higher desire for a fine balance between architectural artifact and the prairie setting, where the continual changes of light, atmosphere, and season heighten the qualities of both the work of art and nature.

The troubled history of the Farnsworth House began at the time of its acknowledged completion in March 1951, when an angry Edith Farnsworth wrote tersely to Mies that

"no further commitments or operations on the Fox River House have my authorization." The originally sympathetic relationship between architect and client (which bordered on romantic love) had deteriorated. Mies justifiably sued for fees. Farnsworth countersued, unjustifiably contesting costs, and lost the case. The house was not fully completed since Mies did not design the furniture he had intended, and Farnsworth, refusing to use existing Mies furniture, "camped out" for years.

The future of the house was first jeopardized in the late 1960s by a lack of vigilance on the part of the State of Illinois. On September 11, 1967, the *Aurora Beacon-News* headline read, "New Bridge May Cause Move for Glass House Owner." This bridge and a new highway were built so close to Farnsworth that the essence of the great country retreat – its surpassing peace and communion with nature – was denatured and rendered unlivable. In 1971, Farnsworth finally moved out of her Fox River house, 20 years after its completion, and sold it to Peter Palumbo (now Lord Palumbo), who acquired it not as a weekend retreat but as another exquisite object in his collection of famous works of architecture, in which he takes great pride.

Palumbo purchased Frank Lloyd Wright's I. N. Hagan House (1954-56), known as Kentuck Knob, at Chalk Hill, Pennsylvania, in 1986 (which, after a fire, he opened to the public in 1996). He rounded out his holdings of houses by 20th-century giants in the late 1980s, when he acquired Le Corbusier's Maison Jaoul, Neuilly (1954-56), which he has since sold. In the early 1960s, inspired by the Seagram Building, Palumbo had persuaded his father, a real estate operator and developer, to commission Mies to design a bronze office tower on a site in the City of London to be called Mansion House Square. (Twenty years later, when that project was refused planning permission by the Minister of the Environment in 1985, Palumbo commissioned Stirling and Wilford to design the building that now stands there.)

At Farnsworth, Palumbo meticulously maintained the white-painted steel structure and its travertine floor, but a flood that inundated the house with almost five feet of water in 1997 necessitated a $250,000 restoration. When Palumbo subsequently opened Farnsworth to the public for a fee, he followed the British Heritage model, filling the house with personal memorabilia and the terrace and grounds with art works from his extensive collection. The natural prairie landscape was transformed into a "gardenesque" clutter inimical to the intentions of Mies.

A series of circumstances again put the house in jeopardy when, in March 2001, ill health and financial difficulties led Palumbo to sell Farnsworth. At first, events moved rapidly. The Friends of the Farnsworth House, formed on April 1, 2001, lobbied the State of Illinois so effectively that on May 31 the state legislature approved a budget expenditure of $7 million to purchase the house. But due to a lethal combination of financial corruption, political infighting, and sloth, by the time of the 2002 gubernatorial election, the check had still not been signed by the incumbent's attorney general. Having failed to win his own bid for the governorship, the same attorney general used the legislative tool of Title Review to kill the Farnsworth property purchase, among others. The new governor's attorney general then claimed that Illinois was in such dire financial straits that the former administration's stalled real-estate purchases were not justifiable.

After the Fox River house had sat on the market for months, Palumbo decided to put it on the auction block. He consigned the sale to Sotheby's, but refused entreaties by the Friends of the Farnsworth House to impose restrictions ensuring that the house would remain in situ. In December 2000, Palumbo had succeeded in securing landmark status for Wright's Hagan House, but he never acted to ensure the same for Mies's Farnsworth House. Anyone could buy it, anyone could move it.

From the outset, the intent for the Seagram Building was to advance the art of architecture and improve the public realm of the city; it was essential, as I wrote to Samuel Bronfman in 1954, to "put up a building which expresses the best of the society in which [we] live, and at the same time the hopes for the betterment of this society. . . . [The] building is not only for the people of [the] company, it is much more for all people, in New York and the rest of the world."[2] From the time it was first occupied in 1958, Seagram was hailed as a masterwork. Lewis Mumford wrote in *The New Yorker* (September 13, 1958) that the building's purity of form and dignity "are almost completely lacking in most contemporary metropolitan architecture, with its endeavor to humanize what is inhuman and to refine what remains so patently vulgar."

As owner and manager, Seagram assumed and maintained a consistent civic role. The company extended a genial permissiveness with respect to the use of open space on the Seagram plaza fronting the building, where the wide marble benches are still favored places for resting beneath the trees or next to the reflecting pools. The play of light and the

2. Phyllis Lambert, letter to Samuel Bronfman, June 28, 1954.

sound of the fountains make the plaza a rare "private" place of quiet and repose in the dense fabric of the city. It also became a rare site for outdoor exhibitions of contemporary sculpture organized by Seagram's curator and the Museum of Modern Art. Furthermore, the Miesian flow of space across the plaza through the glass enclosure and elevator cores revealed the powerful presence of a major work of art in the public domain: Picasso's 1919 curtain for *Le Tricorne*. Seagram's investment in such public amenities extended to either side of the *Tricorne* into the Four Seasons restaurant, designed by Philip Johnson. The ground floor of the building was open to the public, and works of art on paper from Seagram's collection were exhibited in the fourth floor gallery leading to the reception area – as much for the pleasure and edification of the public as for its employees.

As with the Farnsworth House, a change in the ownership of the Seagram Building occurred 20 years after its completion. Because of its unusual financing (the building was never mortgaged), Seagram executives determined in 1978 that it was in the company's best financial interests to sell the building. However, Seagram was determined to ensure the preservation of the building bearing its name, even after its transfer to another owner. At the time, according to New York City Landmarks Preservation Commission regulations, the Seagram Building was 10 years shy of meeting the 30-year age requirement for eligibility.

Seagram and its lawyers developed a creative solution for maintaining the building in its original condition. The company was to remain a major tenant, and the building would continue to be identified with its name. By means of a lease agreement accompanying the sale, Seagram placed restrictions on the new owner. Article 26 of the lease agreement consisted of a series of "thou shalt nots" amounting to absolute prohibitions on changes to the building without prior written consent from the principal tenant. These terms governed changes to the fabric of the building and the use of its public spaces. They were tied to construction documents and undergirded by detailed standards for maintenance. In everyday parlance, the strategy was one of carrot and stick – the carrot being building itself.

On February 15, 1980, the Teachers' Insurance and Annuity Association of America (TIAA) purchased the Seagram Building. The new owners agreed to the provisions of the lease agreement to protect and properly maintain the building; clearly they considered it in their interest to do so. In fact, the restrictions aimed at protecting the building also ensured its future value. Procedures established between Seagram and TIAA worked well, in part due to monitoring by Seagram architects Pasanella and Kline, who were responsible for the maintenance prescriptions of Article 26. According to Article 28 of the same lease agreement, TIAA would seek landmark designation when the building became eligible, and in 1988, 30 years after its opening, the Seagram Building was granted this status. The Four Seasons restaurant, which opened in 1959, was granted the same status in 1993. This unusual instance of a landmarked interior was achieved, however, only after the New York Board of Estimates, exercising a right that now belongs to the City Council, overruled the TIAA's objection that it would restrict future use of the space.

The Seagram Building changed hands again in November 2000, when it was acquired by the German firm RFR Realty. The new ownership has so far been benign. RFR had demonstrated responsible stewardship in the careful restoration of Lever House, which it also owns, but the morphing of the Seagram Company into Seagram Universal in 1995, its subsequent sale to the French water company Vivendi in December 2000, the accompanying name change to Vivendi Universal (VU), and finally, the decision to sell the Seagram Company, have severely compromised Seagram's ability to guarantee the preservation of its architectural legacy. Due to grave financial difficulties caused by the ambitions of VU's now-deposed chairman and chief executive officer, Seagram's successors will no longer rent space in the building when the initial 15-year lease expires in 2005, despite the option to renew for three consecutive 10-year periods. Thus, the provisions agreed to under Article 26 and the close collaboration and philosophical understanding between the original patron (subsequently the chief tenant) and the new owner will be lost. While landmark status will ensure protection against external modifications to the building, who will monitor the quality of maintenance or the integrity and transparency of the curtain wall – from structure to venetian blinds to the three-module-deep luminous ceiling? What is to ensure the continuity of materials and graphics in all public spaces throughout the building, or that edgy works of art and not advertisements appear on the plaza from time to time?

The sale of the Seagram Company thus threatens the future of the Seagram Building. Mies's original intent for the way in which the skeletal-frame office space should be inhabited, so sensitively interpreted by Philip Johnson on Seagram's executive floor, has already been partly obscured by VU's former chairman, and this exemplary installation will no doubt be lost. In the spring of 2003, the Seagram art collections, including paintings, drawings, photographs, and fine drinking vessels dating from the 17th to the 20th centuries, as well as Picasso's *Tricorne* curtain, were put on the auction block – like the Farnsworth House was in December 2003. While it was enormously sad to see the Seagram collection dispersed, the removal of Picasso's *Tricorne* from the building – and therefore the loss of a major public art work – was unthinkable.

After months of public protestation and suspenseful waiting, we now know that the new leadership of Vivendi Universal has recognized the importance of its unique stewardship role. It is VU's intention to donate the *Tricorne* to the city of New York through the New York Conservancy in order that it remain where it is. On December 12, 2003, in another moment of triumph for responsible stewardship, a dramatic Sotheby's sale that lasted only seven minutes ended in the joint purchase of the Farnsworth House by the National Trust and the Landmarks Preservation Council of Illinois, with substantial help from more than 300 individuals – due in large part to the vigilance of the Friends of the Farnsworth House. Farnsworth will not be physically endangered or rendered inauthentic by a move to another site, as was feared, but instead will finally be granted landmark status and full protection under state and federal law.

If the present historical moment has provided grounds for optimism insofar as the Seagram and Farnsworth are concerned, can we hope for a similar form of collective redemption in the rebuilding of the World Trade Center? A week after the Sotheby's sale, Herbert Muschamp wrote in the *New York Times* that the new design for the Freedom Tower at the WTC site has "come closer to being a piece of architecture than the public had the right to expect." This statement followed a roller-coaster ride lasting 20 months, characterized by alternating high and low expectations ever since the Port Authority of New York and New Jersey and the Lower Manhattan Development Corporation solicited proposals for designs in April 2002. The roiling process has involved too many clients with conflicting interests and, most dangerously, assertions over the commercial rights of the lease holder/developer who controls the purse strings. It was inevitable that quarrels would arise among the architects – one chosen in a public competition, the other, privately appointed. Thus again one asks, where is the love that arises from the creation of architecture?

Arguably, the love of architecture resides in the *vox populi*, if anywhere at all. After six commercial schemes were rejected in a process that engaged public opinion, the public sentiment was expressed in a *New York Times* editorial : "When people say they want something splendid in Lower Manhattan – and they say that repeatedly – they mean more than just the memorial itself. They mean that the redevelopment of the larger World Trade Center site should be architecturally ambitious." (May 31, 2002) Does this also imply that it is now the public's responsibility to ensure that buildings like Farnsworth and Seagram, and ultimately the memorial to the World Trade Center, are protected and sustained so that the original architectural idea remains an important mark in the evolution of a shared culture?

Amid the chaos and conflict of private interests today, it would seem that this responsibility does fall to the public agencies of city, state, and federal governments. As we have already seen, only through endlessly repeated expressions of love for architecture on the part of engaged citizens can such agencies be compelled to overcome their usual apathy. Then we might regain clients who, as patrons, demonstrate humility, generosity, kindness, temperance, self-control . . . and love.

PHYLLIS LAMBERT IS THE FOUNDING DIRECTOR OF THE CANADIAN CENTRE FOR ARCHITECTURE IN MONTREAL. SHE STUDIED ARCHITECTURE AT IIT WITH MIES VAN DER ROHE AND WAS INSTRUMENTAL IN HIS SELECTION TO DESIGN THE SEAGRAM BUILDING.

Edward Eigen

Lincoln's Log, or A Tree is Best Measured When it Is Down

"Do you live around here, my boy?" asked Lincoln.

"Yes sir, in Davenport," replied Brayton.

"And what might your name be?" Lincoln went on.

"Brayton, Bud Brayton, they call me," the boy answered; "my dad helped build this railroad."

Lincoln laughed. "Oh, I see," he said.

Then he sat down beside the youth on the end of the bridge ties, with his legs dangling towards the water.

"And I suppose you know all about this river?" he asked.

"Well, I guess I do," was the reply. "It was here when I was born, and – it's been here ever since."

This sally evoked another laugh from the tall stranger.

"Well, well," he said, "I'm mighty glad I walked out here where there is not so much opinion and a little more fact. Now tell me," he went on, "how fast does this water run under here? Have you ever thought of that?"

"No," said young Brayton, "but I know how to find out."

Lincoln smiled kindly down on his companion.

"I knew you did," he said. "Tell me how, will you?"

"Of course," the lad explained, "if you sight the logs and brush coming down the river you'll see they swing out from the island up there about three hundred yards, and then they swing in again right here under the bridge. Have you got a watch?" he asked, turning to his visitor.

"Right here," was the reply, as Lincoln drew a large silver time-piece from his vest pocket.

"Now," exclaimed the boy, "when I spy a log swinging out from the island, I'll tell you, and you can take it again and then we've got the distance and the time. Can't we figure it that way?"[1]

* With this essay, the author recognizes a long-held debt to Emily Roth. Thanks also to Elliot Landry Smith and especially to Sarah Whiting.
1. John W. Starr, Jr., *Lincoln & the Railroads* (New York: Dodd, Mead & Company, 1927), 95–96.

The following essay charts lines of stress that fractured 19th-century America. It limns a map of accidents that marked and remade a (ruined) continent, imagining in some detail the fate of a few machines – rare engines of history, one might say – as they lost control or met with destruction, which usually amounted to the same thing. The idea, at least as it emerges from a cursory examination of the facts, is to question how these accidents fit into the natural order of things. To suggest who or what is responsible for them forms a surprisingly complete account of earth-shaking events, at least in those parts of America where the new steam technology was beginning to extend its imperfectly (self-) regulated force. Which is to say, nearly everywhere, making the accidents of these machines so many sites of intensification – of force and of meaning. This is a preliminary attempt at interpretation; a study pursued further would elevate the term "accident" and its imperfect cognates "disaster" and "catastrophe" to the status of unavoidable structuring agents in the discourse of landscape and history.[2] The epigraph above, reproduced from the biographical study *Lincoln & the Railroads*, serves merely as a point of entry, all such beginnings being more or less fictional. Yet the choice of date seems suitably inauspicious. The 1856 visit of Abraham Lincoln (1809–65) to Davenport, Iowa, corresponds with the publication of James T. Lloyd's *Steamboat Directory, and Disasters on the Western Waters*, its index a morbid litany of ships snagged, exploded, burned, and sunk.[3]

A pretext: on May 6, 1856, the steamship *Effie Afton*, a Louisville-New Orleans packet ship sent north from St. Louis, Missouri, on her first run, struck a bridge spanning the Mississippi from Davenport, Iowa, to Rock Island, Illinois. The bridge had been opened to railroad traffic only two weeks earlier. Allegedly, the *Effie Afton* cleared the draw span and then, one of her side wheels stopping, inexplicably reversed course and drifted back downriver into the bridge's central pier. The ship's galley toppled, setting fire to the vessel, which in turn destroyed the wooden span where it struck. This eyewitness account of the ship's wayward course – no less than of the collision scene – became the subject of intense scrutiny in the legal matter of *Hurd et al. v. Rock Island Bridge Company*. The *Effie Afton*'s owner sought damages from the bridge builder, the Rock Island and Pacific Railroad Company; the Rock Island maintained that the so-called accident was in fact intentional. The motive? It was at Rock Island that the east-to-west course of the railroad, Walt Whitman's "Passage to India," first intersected the storied north-to-south river passage. Lincoln, who as a young man worked as a ferryman – just when steamers were beginning to ply the Ohio and the Mississippi – defended the railroad's right-of-way. Apart from drawing business away from the levees of St. Louis, the steamship operators alleged that the

2. Important steps in this direction are Paul Virilio's *Unknown Quantity* (London: Thames & Hudson, 2003), with its propaedeutic "Museum of Accidents," and David Nye, *The Technological Sublime* (Cambridge: MIT Press, 1994).
3. See James T. Lloyd, *Lloyd's Steamboat Directory, and Disasters on the Western Waters* (Cincinnati: J. T. Lloyd & Co., 1856).

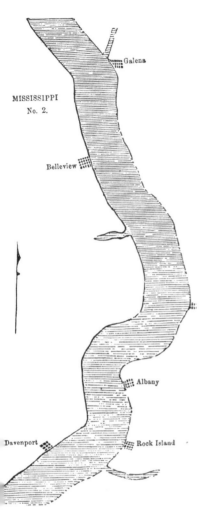

MISSISSIPPI
No. 2.

Galena

Belleview

Albany

Davenport

Rock Island

A STRETCH OF THE MISSISSIPPI IN
WHICH THE *EFFIE AFTON* WENT
DOWN AFTER COLLIDING WITH A
BRIDGE. ILLINOIS IS TO THE RIGHT,
IOWA, TO THE LEFT. FROM *LLOYD'S
STEAMBOAT DIRECTORY*, 1856.

4. See James Corner and Alex MacLean,
*Taking Measures Across the American
Landscape* (New Haven: Yale University
Press, 1996). The practice of offering
credible witness is compellingly discussed
in Steven Shapin and Simon Schaffer,
Leviathan and the Air-Pump (Princeton:
Princeton University Press, 1985).
5. Starr, 99.
6. Leo Marx, *The Pilot and the Passenger*
(New York: Oxford University Press,
1988), 20–22.

railroad bridge created an "obstacle" to navigation. For its part, the Rock Island held that the bridge pier caused no dangerous eddies or crosscurrents in the river; the *Effie Afton*'s was a chance but nonetheless destructive drift.

Thus Lincoln came to Davenport to establish the facts in the matter – after the fact, as it were. He recognized that there was conflicting testimony in the case. Witnesses seldom do agree, especially with regard to the outline of so indistinct an event as an accident in the making. If Lincoln was to reconcile this testimony, he needed to learn "all about this river." The mechanics of fate – or the plot-work of folklore – dictated that 17-year-old Brayton was on hand when Lincoln arrived at Davenport to inspect the bridge built by the boy's father, or rather to observe the river that flowed beneath its span. Initiating their mutual pedagogy in the river, the fast companions set their sights, and Lincoln's large silver timepiece, on the passage of a log around Rock Island. As flowed the log, so must have gone the *Effie Afton*. While always somewhat arbitrary, the art of taking measure is the essence of offering credible witness.[4] In all, during his arguments, Lincoln employed scale-model ships and survey maps to demonstrate "the nature of the [river's] currents, their velocity at certain periods, the custom of navigators and pilots in allowance for drift, the depth of the water at the 'draw' of the bridge, the direction of the piers in relation to the channel, and many other points involving mechanics and engineering."[5] Destined like his father to become an engineer of the Rock Island, Brayton would one day become expert in these data. Yet Lincoln evidently sought to account for a crucial if incalculable factor in his reconstruction of, and assignment of blame for, the accident at Rock Island: the customs of navigators and pilots.

Though immersed in custom, navigation is an "exact science." So Mark Twain insisted in *Life on the Mississippi*, which recounts his own progressive mastery of "the language of this water." In the chapter titled "Continued Perplexities," Twain explains that the Mississippi is a "book that was a dead language to the uneducated passenger." The pilot-house was the classroom in which he studied, ultimately memorizing the river's every trope, as it were. As Leo Marx observes, to become a pilot is to cast a critical eye on the visual pleasures that the river holds in store for the passenger.[6] The river shifts from being a setting of reverie to become "the grimmest and most dead-earnest of reading-matter." Twain writes that:

This sun means that we are going to have wind to-morrow; that

floating log means the river is rising, small thanks to it; that the
slanting mark on the water refers to a bluff reef which is going to
kill somebody's steamboat one of these nights . . . [T]he lines and
circles in the slick water over yonder are a warning that that
troublesome place is shoaling up dangerously; that silver streak in
the shadow of the forest is the 'break' from a new snag, and he has
located himself in the very best place he could have found to fish
for steamboats . . .[7]

7. Mark Twain, *Life on the Mississippi* (New York: Oxford University Press, 1990).
8. Twain, 65.
9. Abraham Lincoln, "Speech to the Jury in the Rock Island Bridge Case, Chicago, Illinois," in *Collected Works of Abraham Lincoln* (New Brunswick: Rutgers University Press , 1953): vol. 417.

The pilot "reads" the lines, circles, and silver streaks, which spell the presence of snags, so-called sawyers (hence the choice of Tom's surname?), which are the death of steamboats. (Evidently the river men who originally mastered the art of governance – or cybernetics – were also the first hermeneutists.) The navigator was instructed to keep a log of his voyage for the benefit of fellow pilots. Sample entry: "Go just outside the wrecks; this is important. New snag just where you straighten down; go above it."[8]

How was the pilot to interpret the unprecedented sight of a railroad bridge fixed permanently in the current of the river? Here was a snag deliberately placed, but not deliberately meant to be a snag. Was the evolution of the steamship's own (countercurrent) force to be directed against it? If Lincoln was to settle these matters in court, he had to address the interrelated questions of what constituted a material obstruction to navigation, and what the phrase "reasonable skill and care" demanded of the navigator. "I differ from them," Lincoln said of the riverboat operators, "in saying that they are bound to exercise no more care than they took before the building of the bridge. If we are allowed by the Legislature to build a bridge, which will require them to do more than before, when a pilot comes along, it is unreasonable for him to dash on, heedless of this structure, which has been legally put there."[9] It was Lincoln's contention that the *Effie Afton*'s pilot had failed to learn the river. The ship arrived at Rock Island on the fifth of May, and lay until the next morning, the day of the accident. Lincoln asked, "When the boat lies up, the pilot has a holiday, and would not any of these jurors have then gone around there, and got acquainted with the place?" That is to say, the jurors are asked to see the river as the pilot does. The pilot needs "information," Lincoln added, precisely what he himself gathered in the aftermath of the accident, beginning with his sighting of a log.

In assigning blame to the *Effie Afton*'s pilot, Lincoln set the exact against the inexact elements of navigational science. "For several days we were entertained with depositions about boats 'smelling a [sand] bar,'" he said, referring to river men's seeming instinct for peril. Yet when the *Effie Afton* got to the center of the very nose she was smelling, "she seems suddenly to have lost her sense of smell and flanks over to the short pier." Was the trail of scent lost or ignored? Relying on river traffic statistics, Lincoln argued that the accident could have been avoided, had the pilot acted on the "information" incumbent upon him to gather during his so-called holiday. To wit, from April 19 to May 6 there were 20 accidents, whereas since that time, there had been but 20 hits and only seven accidents. Thus, "the dangers of this place are tapering off, and, as the boatmen get cool, the accidents get less. We may soon expect, if this ratio is kept up, that there will be no accidents at all." As the railroad's man, Lincoln was paid to trust in such numbers. But for the pilots who knew the river best, the idea that accidents might eventually cease to occur must have appeared so much casuistry. Evidently, something in the nature of the obstruction – its smell – rather than any ascertainable information about it – its measure – directed the (accidental) course of events at Rock Island.

The Rock Island's crossing of the Mississippi was but a sign of things to come. It appears that the river men, trained to read the river like a book, were unable to interpret its meaning. One branch of commerce and communication was poised to replace another, just as the canals had recently replaced the turnpikes. What better proof than Twain's *Life on the Mississippi,* written in 1883 as an elegy for an age of steamboating long since past. Yet the river men's insistence that the bridge posed an obstacle to navigation is perhaps less retrograde than it is symptomatic of a dawning recognition of the perils posed by their own "gross and criminal mismanagement of steam power."[10] The railroads would soon enough command commerce and communication, but the present danger was the very force that drove the railroad's progress and the river's demise.

"They must show reasonable skill and care." The great captain and steamship innovator Henry Miller Shreve was nothing if not confident that his 1821 design of a "machine for sawing snags and sawyers under water" would greatly reduce, if not altogether remove, obstacles from the western rivers. Logs float with the river only to become embedded beneath its surface. In a heroic labor tantamount to felling a forest, Shreve's steam-powered snag boat *Eradicator* cleared the Great Raft from the Red River between 1833–38. This "raft" was not of the fugitive sort upon which Twain's Jim

10. Lloyd, iii.

and Huck were adrift when it was suddenly staved by a giant steamboat. Rather it was an immobile mass of logs that prevented passage of any sort along the river. In this instance, at least, one form of steam technology was clearing the way for another. Notably, Shreve designed the ship's snag beam so that the violent work of removal did not "disturb in the least any of the machinery connected with the boilers or engines."[11] This cautionary measure was no doubt urged upon him by experience with his most famous steamship, the *Washington*. The *Washington*'s innovative flat hull and the mechanics of its high-pressure boiler effectively broke the monopoly of Robert Fulton, the "father of steam boating," on the Mississippi.[12] Yet as was recorded in *Lloyd's Steamboat Directory*, the *Washington*'s boiler exploded on her maiden voyage from Wheeling, Ohio, to New Orleans on June 9, 1816, the furious exhalation of scalding steam taking the lives of seven passengers and three crew members. It was the first steamboat accident in the West. "No human foresight could have anticipated the fatal event," Lloyd wrote.[13]

Shreve and his engineer, who was also injured in the explosion, determined that the fault lay with the engine's safety valves, the operation of which was compromised after the ship accidentally brushed against a sandbar. Inspecting the debris, Shreve saw the way to improving the valves, which, unless disabled, would provide insurance against an explosion. Steamboat operators – particularly on boats whose slower, low-pressure engines were disadvantaged by Shreve's mechanical innovations – often yielded to the temptation to override the safety valve.[14] The increasing frequency of boiler explosions and the mounting toll of victims forced a profound shift in perception: from the obstacles in the way of navigation to the perils posed by navigation itself. Accidents no longer befell steamships; rather, they fulminated from within their own boilers. Legislation was put in place when the mechanical regulator proved ineffective or went unheeded. Not surprisingly, the ship owners argued against regulation, citing their own interest in preserving their boats as the best protection for the traveling public. In any case, following an exceptional spate of disastrous explosions, Congress enacted the Steamboat Act of 1852, a comprehensive measure that not only established standards for the construction, equipment, and operation of steamboat boilers, but prescribed measures for the prevention of fire and collision.[15]

The immediate spur to congressional action was a steamboat accident that would have an incalculable effect upon the future shape of the American landscape. Some possessed of a

11. Henry M. Shreve, "Specifications Forming part of Letters Patent No. 913, Sept. 12, 1838," cited in Edith McCall, *Conquering the Rivers, Henry Miller Shreve and the Navigation of America's Inland Waterways* (Baton Rouge: Louisiana State University Press, 1984), 187.
12. See Louis C. Hunter, "The Invention of the Western Steamboat," *Journal of Economic History*, v. 3, n. 2 (November 1943): 214.
13. Lloyd, 55.
14. See McCall, 147.
15. See George Rogers Taylor, *The Transportation Revolution, 1815–1860* (Armonk: M. E. Sharpe, 1951), 68–69.

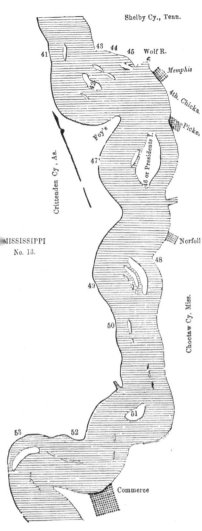

A STRETCH OF THE MISSISSIPPI IN
WHICH THE *SULTANA* WENT DOWN.
TENNESSEE AND MISSISSIPPI ARE TO
THE RIGHT, ARKANSAS IS TO THE
LEFT. FROM *LLOYD'S STEAMBOAT
DIRECTORY*, 1856.

mordant wit might suggest that the effect was in the main salutary. (Based on the facts of the accident alone, Lloyd included it on a list of over three hundred "minor" but fatal disasters.) On July 28, 1852, Andrew Jackson Downing, the promoter of picturesque cottages and rural landscapes, boarded the *Henry Clay* at Newburgh, New York, where he and his brother operated a nursery. Downing's final destination was Washington, D.C., where he was to inspect his design for the National Mall. After pushing off from Newburgh, the crew of the *Henry Clay* resumed their furious stoking of its boilers, for the stop had caused the ship to fall behind the *Armenia*, against which it had been racing since Albany. As on the Mississippi, steam-boating glory on the Hudson was won in such time trials. Just above Kingston the *Henry Clay* passed the *Armenia*, but the strain on its boilers proved too great. One of the boilers caught fire, which quickly spread to the wooden deck and caused the ship to list fatally toward the Yonkers shore. All told, more than 60 lives were lost, including Downing's. In a sign of things to come, a northbound train of the Hudson River Railroad stopped to pick up survivors and the bodies of those who were burned or drowned. The circumstances of the disaster beg the question of whether Downing's romantic vision of the landscape could have survived the coming violence of the Civil War.[16] Another victim of the disaster was Louisa Hawthorne, Nathaniel Hawthorne's sister. As Leo Marx memorably wrote, it was the shriek of a locomotive whistle that assailed Hawthorne while in the woods of Sleepy Hollow in the summer of 1844, and that signaled therewith the intrusion of the machine into the garden.[17]

It is consoling to regard accidents as singular by nature, each requiring a reckoning, if not a remedy. It is possible to name them, to form a mnemonic of despondency. These are the names that head tort cases, that unify a class of the aggrieved. The desire to prevent accidents, however, suggests that there is a pattern to their occurrence. Industrial underwriters sort through wreckage like augurs reading portents. Their actuaries dispassionately log the expected lifespan of man and machine alike. Might accidents not finally be counted among the "most typical and representative things," as Whitman referred to America's vast network of railroad lines and telegraph wires? Far from exceptions, accidents are a consequence of the system. They are everywhere, always lying in wait. In that event, what is a steamship or railroad locomotive but a potential trail of debris leading back – if the trail has not gone cold – to the moment, the

16. See Adam Sweeting, *Reading Houses and Building Books* (Hannover: University Press of New England, 1996), 189.
17. Leo Marx, *The Machine in the Garden: Technology and the Pastoral Ideal in America* (New York: Oxford University Press, 1964), 325.

place, if not finally the cause, of its tragic disarticulation?

But what if the system itself came undone? There was no technological fix for the strife that arose at Rock Island. There was no hope in building a suspension bridge, Lincoln explained to the jury, for none could be built high enough to let the steam stacks pass. Nor was there "hope of burying the issue" and building a tunnel. Lincoln offered that "the proper mood for all parties was to 'live and let live,' and then we will find a cessation of this trouble about the bridge." Two years hence, Lincoln would speak dolefully of "a house divided against itself." The national territory – traversed by corridors both natural and artificial – was divided into free and slave-holding latitudes. How to steer clear of the impasse? Lincoln would dismantle the legal scaffolding, the divisive "machinery," as he called it, of the Dred Scott decision and the Nebraska Doctrine. He proposed to begin by taking measure of the "flowing," as he had already done not long ago by sighting a log.[18] "If we could first know where we are, and wither we are tending, we could better judge what to do, and how to do it."[19] The hour was nigh to exercise reasonable skill and care.

"Oh Captain! My Captain!" In the wake of Lincoln's assassination on Good Friday, April 14, 1865, Secretary of War Edwin M. Stanton planned the route and itinerary of the series of trains that would convey Lincoln's body home to Springfield, Illinois. After lying in state in the rotunda of the Capitol, Lincoln's body was escorted to the Baltimore and Ohio railroad depot on the morning of April 21, 1865. The train started promptly from the station at eight o'clock with the engine bell tolling. Starr noted that its rate of speed was limited to "avoid accidents," and that during the entire journey to Springfield it was preceded by a pilot engine to ensure that the way was clear. The domed rotundas of city halls and state capitols were so many solemn stations in the funeral's progress. In Albany, "every train, boat, and omnibus leading into the city was crowded with people wishing to pay their last tribute of respect"; in Buffalo, the open casket was viewed at an estimated rate of 180 persons per minute.[20] As Lincoln's Funeral Train made its northwest passage, word of his death was broadcast along the lower Mississippi by the great side-wheel steamer *Sultana*.[21] On April 21, as Lincoln's train departed Washington, the *Sultana* embarked on a scheduled run to New Orleans.

"The port is near." After taking on passengers and cargo in New Orleans, the *Sultana*'s return to Cairo was halted at Natchez to makes repairs to its balking engine. Proceeding

18. On "Flowing," see F. O. Mathiessen, *American Renaissance* (New York: Oxford University Press, 1941), 64–70.
19. Abraham Lincoln, "Certified Transcript of Passage from the House Divided Speech," in *Collected Works of Abraham Lincoln*, v. 4: 147.
20. Starr, 271.
21. William O. Bryant, *Cahaba Prison and the Sultana Disaster* (Tuscaloosa: University of Alabama Press, 1990), 119.

upriver to Vicksburg, the *Sultana* took on more than 2,000 newly released Union inmates from the Confederate prisons at Cahaba and Andersonville. These soldiers were never to be repatriated. On April 27, about seven miles above Memphis, working against unusually heavy spring flood waters, the *Sultana*'s overcharged boilers exploded. In the worst maritime disaster in United States history, 1,238 lives were lost. Lincoln's Funeral Train continued its homeward passage, arriving one hour late in Springfield on May 3, "and the journey, so far as the railroad was concerned, was over."[22]

Around the turn of the century, accounts circulated that Booker T. Washington was behind an effort to restore the Funeral Car, the hulk of which was found in an Omaha, Nebraska, rail yard. Said to have been designed to allow Lincoln to visit the battle front, the car was described as "iron-clad," as if evoking the class of submarine ships that first saw action during the Civil War. The myth evolved with the ascendancy of the railroad. Sigfried Giedion, that Herodotus of the machine age, held that the conveyance was a Pullman sleeper car, its use as Lincoln's hearse earning good publicity for its coachbuilder.[23] Following salvage operations and an inconclusive investigation of the destruction of the *Sultana*, the ship, along with the age of the steamship, was largely forgotten. It lived on, though, in the corporate lore of the Hartford Insurance and Steam Boiler Inspection Company, the industrial underwriter whose founding was inspired by the accident. Yet the varying course of the Mississippi eventually flowed east of the wreck, burying its remains beneath twenty feet of mud.[24]

22. Starr, 274.
23. See Sigfried Giedion, *Mechanization Takes Command* (New York: Oxford University Press, 1948), 453. According to Starr, the car was built under the authority of the United States Military Railroad in the car shops inside the stockade at Alexandria, Virginia. Lincoln refused to accept the lavishly appointed car, or to ride in it during his lifetime. See Starr, 277.
24. See Gene Eric Salecker, *Disaster on the Mississippi* (Annapolis: Naval Institute Press,1996), 209.

EDWARD EIGEN WAS BORN NEAR BROOKLYN, NEW YORK. HE CURRENTLY TEACHES THE HISTORY AND THEORY OF ARCHITECTURE AND LANDSCAPE AT THE SCHOOL OF ARCHITECTURE, PRINCETON UNIVERSITY.

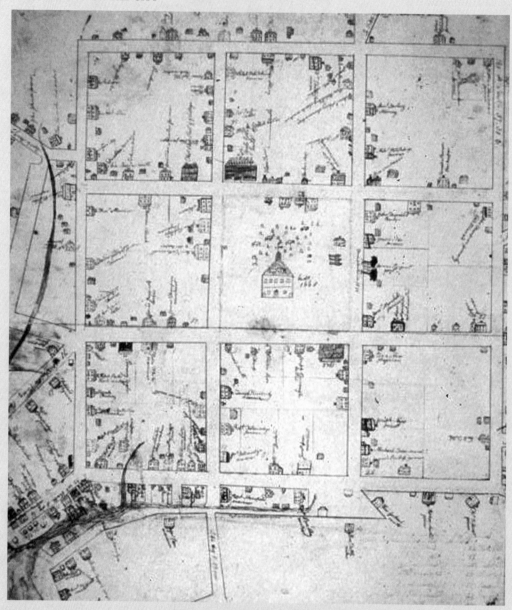

NEW HAVEN, CONNECTICUT, CITY PLAN, 1748 (DETAIL). THE CENTER SQUARE IS TODAY THE NEW HAVEN GREEN, NOW DIVIDED ASYMMETRICALLY BY ONE STREET. COLLECTION OF THE YALE UNIVERSITY LIBRARIES.

Breakfasting in the Omni Hotel's top-floor dining room, overlooking the New Haven Green, one thinks, just how big is this carpet of lawn? And even more, how has it managed to remain a true New England town green all these decades? A reproduction of a 1748 map of the city's original nine-square-grid layout hangs adjacent to the view, providing a simple explanation for what lies below. It turns out the green is 17 acres, bisected by one street and "built up" with several churches. That's one more acre than the World Trade Center site in New York. And pause for thought.

—The Log Team

John Huddleston

Killing Ground

Killing Ground is excerpted from Killing Ground: Photographs of the Civil War and the Changing American Landscape, *published by Johns Hopkins University Press. The original contemporary photographs were made in color.*

The American Civil War is often called the first modern war because of the large number of casualties – 620,000 dead – compulsory military service, the use of longer-range weaponry, ironclad waterships, trenches, and scorched-earth policies against the civilian population. Extensive photographic coverage was also new, breaking painting's long and popular tradition of the glorious depiction of warfare.

The impetus for this project came from living near Civil War battlefields and experiencing their beauty and power from an early age. My father's military knowledge and presence brought substance to the events that took place on those fields. I felt excitement, chaos, pain. I felt repsect for the sacrifice and heroism of the soldiers, and I felt fear of having life itself so removed from one's control. These emotions coexisted with the serenity and physical beauty of the land.

A major emphasis of this project is the resonance of history in the landscape. Are physical and spiritual traces of the great slaughter still present in these places? Remains of blood and bodies, as well as the instruments of their destruction – the lead of the Minié balls and the iron of the artillery rounds – still exist in the earth. Much of the land was physically altered with the construction and destruction of defensive earthworks, whose weathered remains are clearly visible.

Spiritual traces are more elusive. The search for the latent energies of these battlefiels inevitably leads back to histories, metaphors, and myths. The tensions and sufferings of the soldiers involved in the riotous circumstance of these locations 140 years ago may come to us through written descriptions, the color of the soil, or collective memory.

The Civil War images inform my photographs. In coupling the historical photographs with my own images, I sought wide-ranging connections of culture, politics, economics, and environment. Both sets of photographs were made by searching for the traces of war. The Civil War photographers searched for visual material after the action in order to examine what had happened. Proximate in time, they produced dynamic photographs of immediate consequences. Much later in time, I have made photographs more concerned with the long-term results.

JOHN HUDDLESTON IS A PROFESSOR OF ART AT MIDDLEBURY COLLEGE. HIS PHOTOGRAPHS HAVE BEEN WIDELY EXHIBITED AND HAVE APPEARED IN HARPER'S, PRESERVATION, WORTH, AND DOUBLETAKE.

Rappahannock Station, Virginia.
Site of the Confederate Center.

Rappahannock Station, Virginia,
November 7, 1863. After the bat-
tle, in which there were 2,049
American casualties, Union
engineers made their camp here.
Photo: Timothy O'Sullivan;
Eaton, *Original Photographs
Taken on the Battlefields*, 80.

PETERSBURG, VIRGINIA.
SITE OF FORT SEDGWICK.

Petersburg, Virginia. The bombproof quarters of Fort Sedgwick, a key position on the eastern Union siege line from June 15, 1864 – April 2, 1865. Photo: Timothy O'Sullivan and Alexander Gardner; Prints and Photographs Division, Library of Congress.

Nashville, Tennessee. Union
defensive line at Nashville on
the second day of battle,
December 15-16, 1864. Photo:
George N. Bernard; Prints and
Photographs Division, Library
of Congress.

Nashville, Tennessee. Site
of the Union attack on the
Confederate Left, which led
to 7,407 casualties.

Chancellorsville, Virginia, May 1–4 1863, where 30,051 American casualties were sustained. This Confederate position below Marye's Heights was photographed within a half-hour of their retreat. Photo: Andrew J. Russell; Prints and Photographs Division, Library of Congress.

CHANCELLORSVILLE, VIRGINIA. THE
FIRST CONTACT BETWEEN THE
ARMIES OCCURRED HERE, WHERE A
HOUSING DEVELOPMENT WILL SOON
BE BUILT.

Librarians and archivists are meticulous loggers. Last November (that is, November 22, 2003), the Avery Architectural and Fine Arts Library at Columbia University honored retiring director Angela Giral with a symposium: "Documenting Architecture in the 21st Century." The conference was academic in nature; representatives from institutions such as New York's Museum of Modern Art and the Massachusetts Institute of Technology discussed the theoretical implications of architectural monographs, periodicals, drawings, and archival materials, rather than dealing with technical problems and solutions.

C. Ford Peatross, architecture curator at the Library of Congress, reflected his generation's anxiety over documenting the digital when he asked Giral to "take me with you!" Given the constant advance of technology, libraries must both maintain obsolete software and continually acquire new systems and new interpreters of those systems. Librarians at the symposium were concerned about access, since allowing students and researchers firsthand access to architectural documents gives the archives meaning. Jeffrey Cohen, an architectural historian, proposed an architectural archive database to meet the needs of the generations who do not trust information that cannot be found on Google. Though infinitely reproducible and distributable, digital information lacks the physical authenticity of paper documentation. Architect Laurie Hawkinson worried about distinguishing "originals" from updated versions.

The attitude of the elder archivists toward the digitized future was best summarized by Phyllis Lambert, founding director of the Canadian Centre for Architecture, which houses extraordinary archives. She clipped the conference short with a terse response to the final presentation on digital archiving: "Just so you know, there are people, librarians, working on this, so we don't have to talk about it." The respondent took his cue to end the discussion and move on to the wine reception. Indeed, the Art Institute of Chicago has hired a consultant to define standard methods for archiving digital information, hoping to reach a conclusive plan of action by fall 2004.

– Larissa Babij

Timothy Hyde

For Dummies Turns To Architecture

Surely the most conclusive evidence of architecture's acceptance into the American cultural mainstream is not the proliferation of shelter magazines or the public fascination with the Lower Manhattan Development Corporation's design competition for the World Trade Center site but the publication of *Architecture for Dummies*. The well-known and invaluable *For Dummies* series – "over 100 million *Dummies* books in print" – provides surveys of every subject worthy of general interest, and now architecture has joined topics that run from *Chemistry for Dummies* to *Candle and Soap Making for Dummies*.[1]

1.Readers who have already purchased *Candle and Soap Making for Dummies* should be advised that the Consumer Products Safety Commission has issued a recall of this book. The book includes instructions for making lye, but specifies the incorrect sequence for combining sodium hydroxide and water, which may cause the mixture to erupt. Readers of *Chemistry for Dummies* would no doubt have spotted this error on their own.

The books provide basic facts presented in clear, self-consciously unthreatening prose. No "silly details," no "useless background information," no jargon, just straight-to-the-point presentations written in "plain English" (see *English Grammar for Dummies*). The excitement of the new *Architecture for Dummies* lies in the promise of just such a rendition of architecture – architecture reduced to its bare facts, to clearly stated, comprehensible principles that reveal, as the cover guarantees, "the thrill of architecture from the Great Pyramids to the Guggenheim Bilbao." It is to Deborah Dietsch's credit that she has even attempted to write such a book, let alone successfully finished it.

So, one might ask, what is the essence of architecture, and why do we need *Architecture for Dummies*? Robert A. M. Stern, in his foreword to the book, preempts Dietsch on these questions, providing six affirmations of what architecture is, and two declarations of what it is not: "Architecture is an artistic and practical expression of the real world – it is the art of building in the service of individuals and institutions. It is the art of construction, not deconstruction; of representation, not communication; it is the solidity of the here-and-now. Architecture is important. It is the setting for life." Of course, telling the *Dummies* reader that architecture is not "deconstruction" or "communication" without explaining that those words don't just provide a nice turn of phrase but reference broad positions in architectural culture breaks the *For Dummies* rules. Slipping in this jargon-in-disguise is poor manners on Stern's part (see *Etiquette for Dummies*).

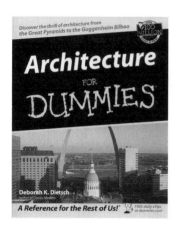

ARCHITECTURE FOR DUMMIES,
BY DEBORAH K. DIETSCH. WILEY
PUBLISHING INC., 2002. 308 PAGES,
ORIGINAL IN PAPER. $21.99 US.

2. The first line of this Paul Simon song
is, "'The problem is all inside your head,'
she said to me." (See *Songwriting for
Dummies*.)

Having asserted the self-evident "reality of architecture," Stern explains why people don't already understand it. The answer, of course, is theory and its obfuscations, but he ascribes a particular and peculiar motivation to the theorists: "Architecture is a field whose very nature is endlessly questioned by its own practitioners and appointed experts – theorists and critics, who, to avoid confronting the simple but profound circumstances of architecture, try to judge it by criteria outside itself, whether from literature or science or the social sciences, or whatever." Describing this behavior as a "process of avoidance" and invoking the song "Fifty Ways to Leave your Lover,"[2] Stern makes clear his belief that theorists and critics are both delusional and in denial. But confirming such a determination would obviously require recourse to realms of expertise outside of architecture (see *Psychology for Dummies*).

No matter, says Stern, because "architecture can stand on its own." With this phrase, he updates some well-pedigreed advice – "to thine own self be true" was the bard's way of putting it (see *Shakespeare for Dummies*). In fact, the pertinent model of avoidance is clearly not Paul Simon's hapless lover, but Hamlet, who circles ineffectually around the "profound circumstance" of which he is all too aware. It must be admitted that theorists do have a suspicious sympathy for Hamlet. But one must also keep in mind that the earnest advice quoted above is one of the litany of truisms spoken by Polonius – which is to say, it is no doubt true, but completely beside the point.

What of the book itself? Here Dietsch takes charge, "sweeping away the cobwebs spun by theoreticians to reveal the simple but fascinating lessons of architecture." Several predictable criticisms could be offered: omissions, inaccuracies, and irrelevancies are all risks of the format. Dietsch's reduction of Latin American architecture to Mesoamerican pyramids and Barragán's colored walls may merely reflect the conventional marginalization of that region (see *World History for Dummies* and *Geography for Dummies*). Or when Dietsch writes of the Bibliothèque Ste.-Geneviève – "Recalling the architecture of a train station, the cast-iron structure symbolized the reader's journey into the world of knowledge. Pretty neat, huh?" – she may have been drawn across the line of oversimplification by her mandate to be accessible and funny. But these are the kinds of pedantic criticisms Polonius would make.

One could also criticize the photographs included in the book, which are appallingly bad (see *Photography for Dummies*).

The tilted horizon line of the image of St. Peter's makes the building appear to be sinking, and an interior photograph of Soane's House is underexposed to the point of illegibility. In the cover photograph, a view looking east over St. Louis, Saarinen's Gateway Arch frames the dome of the Old Courthouse; but the body of the Courthouse is cut off, as is the top of the Arch; a high-rise obscures the southern leg of the Arch, and the industrial background landscape fills the center of the picture. The motivation behind these odd selections (most obtained from www.GreatBuildings.com) is undoubtedly the avoidance of copyright fees (see *Patents, Copyrights, and Trademarks for Dummies*). But the images, by disrupting the pure profundity of the architectural object, have an unexpected advantage, presenting something much nearer to an actual experience than, say, a Julius Shulman photo. The clutter that obscures the architecture in St. Louis is in fact what the *Dummies* reader will find there.

Upon arriving in St. Louis, that reader can take advantage of Dietsch's method for deciding "Is This Architecture Any Good?" Good architecture can be established with affirmative answers to six questions: "Does it express its function in a visually intriguing way? Does it complement or contrast with its surroundings? Is it well built? Does it continue to age well? Does it have the ability to surprise, inspire, delight, or disturb you? Is it simply unforgettable?"[3] In order to draw conclusions using these commonsense guidelines, the reader must still ponder whether the answer is yes or no.

Dietsch addresses this problem first with a ten-page primer on "How to Look at a Building," notable for its unacknowledged debt to another Dane, Steen Eiler Rasmussen. Dietsch names nine design fundamentals – "solids, voids, scale, massing, proportion, rhythm, color, texture, and light" – that reflect the influence of Rasmussen's book *Experiencing Architecture*.[4] This similarity makes one realize that *Experiencing Architecture* should itself be recognized as an earlier and formidable *Architecture for Dummies*. Indeed, in his preface, Rasmussen specifies his desire to present architecture "simply and clearly" so that "even an interested teenager might understand it," with the intention of "arousing interest in and understanding of the work the architect does." A detailed comparison of the two books and their respective determinations on how to address an uninformed reader – or "amateur" in Rasmussen's polite phrase – cannot be undertaken here, but would certainly provide further grist for the decline-of-culture industry in academic and political circles.

3. On this last question, see also *Improving Your Memory for Dummies*.
4. The chapters in *Experiencing Architecture* include Solids and Cavities in Architecture, Scale and Proportion, Rhythm in Architecture, Color in Architecture, Textural Effects, Daylight in Architecture, and Hearing in Architecture (this last subject, sound, is included in Dietsch's primer as well).

Following the primer model, Dietsch gives brief descriptions of the profession and structures, and then an account of architectural history that takes up two-thirds of her book. In spite of inevitable omissions, these sections amount to a survey impressive for being as comprehensive as it is concise, and Dietsch manages a succinct tag line for the significance of any given building or architectural *œuvre* (see *French for Dummies*). The essence of Wright's architecture, for example, is "horizontality," while Borromini's consists of "fluidity" and "undulation."

One could make an architectural parlor game out of the scrutiny of this survey – who gets more of the precious stock of pages, and so on[5] – but their real interest lies in whether they can possibly succeed in conveying, in Stern's words, "the lessons of architecture." Captions such as "horizontality" have only the appearance of complete lucidity; they are written in plain English and are reasonably accurate, but do not by themselves reveal the significance of the architecture they describe. For example, in the accounts of the Hagia Sophia and De Stijl architecture, the noteworthy characteristic of the former is that its completed dome "appeared to float miraculously," while in the latter, that walls and planes "seemed to hover in space." Clear enough, but how does one distinguish the relevant meanings of these two instances of levitation? (For the answer, see, respectively, *Religion for Dummies* and *Art for Dummies*.) Similarly, after learning that both the ancient Egyptians and the Mayans built pyramids, how does one decide what distinctions to draw between them (see *Mythology for Dummies*)? Or to return to St. Louis, cheat sheet in hand, won't further knowledge of Lewis and Clark or the Dred Scott trial assist in the contemplation of the Gateway Arch and the Old Courthouse (see *U.S. History for Dummies*[6])?

At other points, Dietsch deliberately includes facts with little apparent relevance to profound architectural lessons, as in her list of the "Ten Most Fascinating Architects Working Today."[7] Here again, a succinct phrase distills the character of contemporary work – "dynamic energy" for Zaha Hadid, "transparency and light" for Jean Nouvel, and so on – but given the requirement for no-frills writing, it's unclear why Dietsch insists on places and dates of birth. With time and space at a premium, what exactly does the reader glean from the knowledge that Predock "was born in 1936 in Lebanon, Missouri"? (See, perhaps, *Astrology for Dummies*.)

The reason, of course, is accessibility, the need to draw the *Dummies* reader into the story of architecture. This is

5. It's Mies, with 85 lines of text, to Wright's 72; Corb is a trailing third with 65, and no one else comes close (see *Everyday Math for Dummies*).
6. More detailed knowledge can be gleaned from the recently published *Lewis and Clark for Dummies* and *The Civil War for Dummies*.
7. Ando, Diller & Scofidio, Gehry, Hadid, Herzog & de Meuron, Koolhaas, Libeskind, Nouvel, Piano, Predock. (Predock's back-cover blurb gives exorbitant praise for Dietsch's authorship. See *Getting Results for Dummies*.)

also the reason for the icons inserted alongside the text, a standard component of the *For Dummies* brand intended to clarify and categorize information, identifying Lingo, Technical Stuff, and Historical Notes. The Technical Stuff icon, to denote "information related to building construction and technology," appears next to passages such as detailed descriptions of the cables on the Brooklyn Bridge, but it also accompanies the following statement about the Salk Institute: "The light-filled stage, with its view toward the sea and the horizon beyond, poetically symbolizes the institute's mission of researching the mysteries of nature."

This would seem to be less of a technical description (but see *Technical Writing for Dummies* to be sure), and it could be a mistake – or perhaps the insight of a *For Dummies* editor responsible for scanning the text to find icon-appropriate passages. But one would do better to accept that this kind of description is indeed Technical Stuff, a specifically architectural way of talking. *Architecture for Dummies* reveals, in its successful distillation, that the appreciation of architecture requires coming to terms with it by drawing out relationships to other forms of experiences – most of them fortunately already covered by another title in the *For Dummies* series.

So, yes, architecture can indeed stand on its own, but why would it want to? Proverbial statements about what architecture "is" are beside the point, less important than its negotiations with other modes of knowledge. After all, Hamlet's most famous question, contrary to its appearance, is not ontological but epistemological (see *Philosophy for Dummies*). All those critics and theorists rattle about Elsinore, wringing their hands in agonized indecision; Polonius, meanwhile, has his answers at the ready. By the end of the play, of course, Hamlet and everyone else have shuffled off their mortal coils – but Polonius is dead before the end of the Third Act.

TIMOTHY HYDE IS AN ARCHITECT, THEORIST, HISTORIAN, AND FATHER OF TWINS (SEE *PARENTING FOR DUMMIES*).

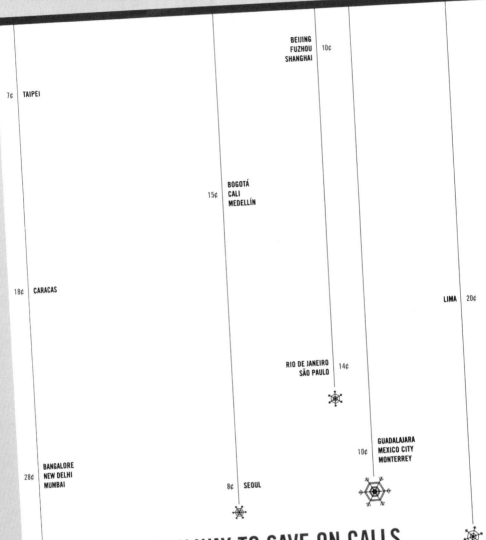

BEIJING
FUZHOU   10¢
SHANGHAI

7¢   TAIPEI

BOGOTÁ
15¢   CALI
MEDELLÍN

18¢   CARACAS   LIMA   20¢

RIO DE JANEIRO   14¢
SÃO PAULO

GUADALAJARA
10¢   MEXICO CITY
MONTERREY

BANGALORE
28¢   NEW DELHI
MUMBAI   8¢   SEOUL

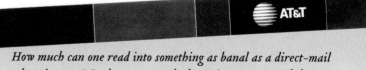

HERE'S A NEW WAY TO SAVE ON CALLS
TO FAMILY AND FRIENDS AROUND THE WORLD

AT&T

How much can one read into something as banal as a direct-mail advertisement? Perhaps a great deal. AT&T's "map" of the world seems to suggest several new geographies: new longitudinal alignments, territories separated by only a few cents, maps of migrating populations wanting to phone home. Has the time come to formally recognize the advertising industry as contemporary cartographers? – The Log Team

Chantal Thomas
*Translated from the
French by Julie Rose*

From Proust
To the Mobile Phone

1. GO AND PHONE

In 1899, there were seven thousand telephone subscribers in Paris and its environs. Possession of such a rare and precious object demonstrated class privilege or the favor of fortune, or else it was a more or less compulsory attribute of professional activity. Doctors' rooms and cafés, for instance, had them. When it was really important to be reachable by telephone and you couldn't have the magic medium yourself, you located yourself in convenient proximity to someone who did. When he was forced to move house, Odilon Albaret, a taxi driver in the 1910s, accordingly sought an apartment close to a café, which was not easily done in the suburbs of the times. Even more difficult, the café had to be open late at night so that he could receive the calls made by his customers, who were invariably insomniac night owls. There weren't many of them, but one who regularly called around midnight – by far his best customer – went by the name of Marcel Proust. And so it was that in relocating his nest, Monsieur Albaret was guided by the presence of a telephone from which Monsieur Proust's messages could be passed on to him. This was deemed perfectly logical. Just as a person might decide today to live as close as possible to the metro, then you went to the phone. The phone did not come to you, even if equipped with a spiral cord.

To go and phone was effectively one of the main chores of Odilon's young wife, Céleste Albaret, after she went to work for Proust. In her reminiscences, *Monsieur Proust*, Céleste evokes her first moments in Paris, recalling how *everything knocked her out* at the time, country girl that she was.[1] *Everything* included not only the shock of the big city, with its crowds and clamor, but also the astounding discovery of Proust's universe – his mania for ritual, his exclusively nocturnal life. Little by little, moreover, the apartment on Boulevard Haussmann, that microcosm that so fascinated her, blocked out the rest of the world. Its silence and eternal night were to absorb Céleste's destiny.

Céleste is the one who ensures communication between this "navire night" – made absolutely subject to the œuvre to be accomplished – and the outside world, which exists only

1. See Céleste Albaret, *Monsieur Proust* (New York: New York Review of Books, 2003) for most recent English translation.

65

in relation to the œuvre. It is only in this connection that the world sometimes remains useful, if not strictly necessary. Proust needs a piece of information, confirmation of his memory; he needs to see someone again: "I'd made up my mind not to go out again, but I think I'd quite like to see Princess Soutzo. We'll have to phone her to see if I can pay her a call." This might be very late, the middle of the night; yet Céleste rushes off and quickly throws on some clothes to go down to the café that stays open late, at the corner of Rue de la Pépinière and Rue d'Anjou. It might be during the wartime night curfew, but she doesn't hesitate for a second. She knows there is nothing capricious about Proust's request. It corresponds to a gap in the manuscript to which he dedicates himself, body and soul. The person she must telephone is part of a scene, a sentence. And when Proust goes out to pay this person a visit, it is only in appearance that he abandons the internal music of the words he has written. In reality, he will still be there, within his text. It is only to serve the latter that he makes the immense effort of getting out of bed. Céleste understands this: serving Proust and serving the text of *À La Recherche du temps perdu* amount to the same thing – whether it means going to phone or putting his papers in order. "Don't forget to phone the people I mentioned and to tidy up my notes," he would tell her in a voice that remains forever unknown to us, and with a diction that I imagine as clear and elegant – a diction that takes its time.

In the same burst of imagination, vain but irresistible, I imagine that his words had the same assurance and mastery as his faultless syntactical virtuosity – the virtuosity that allowed him to juggle with dependent clauses and keep piling up relative propositions without losing sight of the central idea. I'm certain that his spoken word, far from being reduced to a smattering of phrases shot out randomly like tiny bunches of confetti, had the dazzling allure of an arborescence that we watch grow and flourish. Something that, though very clear and even transparent, is elaborated between the person speaking and the person listening, looping across the distance from one to the other. That Proust played, out loud, as an artist with all the resources of the French language, I can well imagine without too much risk of being wrong. But I'm inventing his laugh, a laugh that took hold of him sometimes when he suddenly decided to read a few pages of his manuscript to a friend.

On the other hand, he isn't laughing when he verifies that Céleste can rattle off the names and phone numbers of his friends and that she has retained the messages to be transmitted. "In the beginning," Céleste says, "he made me repeat his messages very carefully. He didn't need to do this for long. I truly had become his own personal recorder – to such an extent that people mistook us over the phone and would say to me 'Hello? What? Oh, it's you, Marcel? How wonderful!'"

But despite such proof, Proust couldn't stop himself from checking up: "Even when he knew he could count on my faithfully repeating his words, he just could never give up policing me, though he'd try and pretend he wasn't. At such times, he wouldn't look at me – which was very rare with him when he spoke. He would listen to me repeat his words and, when I had finished, he would turn toward me with a sweet smile and say, 'Thank you, that's absolutely right. Please forgive me for having asked. I'm so tired, I'd almost forgotten myself.' But I knew what I was dealing with. Despite all his trust, he had had his doubts. He couldn't rest until I had repeated the lesson I'd learned by heart."

On this point, Proust was never completely reassured. Though Céleste's memory was exceptional, her fear of forgetting led her to keep a list of important names on a piece of cardboard that she carried with her at all times, and even that was never enough to lay Proust's doubts to rest. She knew all the names by heart and, even more than the names, she had Proust's voice in her head: "I carried his voice around with me, in a way." As a faithful messenger, she was able to reproduce *exactly* both the contents of the message and the voice that had dictated it. She was the delegated presence of her master – her master's voice – which the telephone served to transmit. There is continuity between the delegated use of the phone and the delivery of messages by hand: Céleste relays purely practical messages, nothing more.

Proust can't laugh in his anxiety that Céleste might distort or forget a bit of his message. He laughs even less when, at the very beginning of the young woman's entry into his service, he notes that she has never used a telephone before in her life. She's unlikely even to have laid eyes on one. Perhaps she has seen one a few meters away, on the other side of the glass, inside a café. But all of the sudden, it's her turn and she panics. Proust teaches her what to say: "Do I indeed have the honor of speaking to Monsieur, the count of . . . , to Monsieur X or to Madame Y?"

In those days there was still a telephone in Proust's apartment. Later on he would have it cut off. The noise of its ringing annoyed him even at a distance, even when muffled by the cork tiles and thick curtains that protected his bedroom.

He wanted to hear voices other than those of his characters. For him, the telephone was a two-edged sword: a means of contact with the outside world, but one that must never compromise the fervent endeavor to keep the silence. Proust was deadly serious about phoning. The telephone, for him, was never a light matter.

This seriousness commands our attention because it speaks, in exemplary fashion, to the demands of Proust's writing. But we might well ask ourselves, only to his writing? Or more generally to the demands of his thought, of that inner life without which we are all mere puppets jerked about by chance circumstances, the chain of events? The silence of the Proustian bedroom has nothing to do with deafness; it is the silence that allows us to hear ourselves think.

2. GOING PHONING

A century later, at the beginning of the third millennium, there is nothing more banal than having a telephone in one's home. No one goes out to phone unless on holiday or out on the town, and even that is a thing of the past since the spread of the mobile phone. As its name suggests, the mobile phone goes with us, accompanies our every move. It is the accessory that goes with our freedom to come and go in the world. The ads trumpet: "A *nomad*, not a commitment. Choose independence." Alternatively: "Sets that leave your hands free. You no longer have to choose between driving and talking on the phone." The practical advantages of the mobile phone are obvious (to say nothing of its success as an aesthetic object, its toylike compactness, its lightness). I can call from anywhere at anytime. And I can only be reached if I want to be. What could be better?

The slavery of sitting by the phone waiting for that special call and the Pavlovian jump up when it starts ringing are both a thing of the past. Jean Cocteau used to scoff: "I'm not some servant you ring and who comes running when called." The cord has been cut. The mobile phone makes us masters of the game in our relationships with family and friends. In certain jobs, it simplifies the conditions of work astonishingly.

But is the cord cut? Do we really no longer jump when called? Are we no longer systematically forced to answer? Everywhere you look today you see people who, certainly, are not running when they're called, but rather are endlessly patting themselves, feeling for the location of the ringing, where *they* are ringing. Recall that marvelously scandalous bit of poetry that occurs in Genet's play, *Le Balcon*, when the general says: "I was snowing." It ceases to be scandalous or poetic in the formula, "*I was ringing, I am ringing, we are ringing.*" This is neither a rite of celebration nor an impromptu spectacle. It's every man for himself. We are not ringing in unison. "Hello. Yes. It's me . . . It's me, yes . . . I can hardly hear you . . . Where am I? At the Quai de la Marine, what about you? . . . Right opposite on the church steps? Oh, yeah, I can see you!"

It's ringing everywhere, and in some places, all the time. In railway stations, for instance. Everywhere, people are talking to themselves, whether standing or having just sat down in the train. Dozens and dozens of people are all saying at the same time, "I'm at the Gare de Lyon, I'll be there at ten past twelve." "Listen, we're in the TGV. Everything's OK. I tried to get you a moment ago, but you didn't answer. We get in at five to six. Love you. Catch you later." To say nothing of the people telling absolute whoppers, lying with impunity, in public.

At the airport they talk right up until the plane takes off, nattering on endlessly to overcome separation – whether tenderly saying goodbye or fighting like cats and dogs. Fusion or fury, it amounts to the same thing. Around six in the evening, on the commute between the office and home, in that indeterminate time when a crumb of the unanticipated can gum up the works, something makes you deviate from your path. So you hook up. You connect. You get anxious: "I thought I'd ring you in case you were trying to ring me this morning, because I went out without my mobile." You warn: "I'm approaching Filles du Calvaire station. I'll be home in ten minutes." "I'm on my way, I'll grab some bread." "I'm on my way . . . I'm here."

People walk with their phones in their hands, as though they were an extension of a self that has abandoned the wandering and freedom that the stroll – the trip –permits. The phone, not so much mobile as portable (though the way people walk around blind and deaf to everything around them, literally hanging on the phone, one might well wonder who is carrying whom), is an apparatus designed to destroy solitude: "Always reachable, never really alone: this is the great fantasy of subscribers," said a recent magazine headline. Journalist Brigitte Benkemoun continues, "If they are made to wait five minutes outside at a café, you won't find them combing through their diaries or the drinks menu anymore. No way. These days they take out their cell phones and start punching in the numbers! Whether in a car, a taxi, or on the bus, dreaming idly as the miles file past is finished. And portables seem even more vital for singles. 'It's a way of seizing every opportunity,' confides Sonia, thirty-seven.

'There might be an invitation to dinner, or friends might offer me a ticket to a concert at the last minute. . . . Without my portable, I'd be on my own a lot more.'"

The portable is conceived as "an anti-stress device" and, as a result, is highly valued by women. According to another magazine, *Mobiles,* "Women remain reachable and can call anywhere, anytime, so they feel reassured. . . . And for mothers who are slightly anxious, it relieves their consciences: they can go out and have a drink while remaining contactable in case of an emergency. Providers have certainly picked up on this maternal aspect and special deals for children and teenagers are equally aimed at mothers, who are reassured by being able to call their offspring wherever they are."

The rampant mania for the portable phone is spectacular: more than twenty million users in France and four billion throughout the world, and growing. While taken as a sign of liberation, this trend in fact reveals a degree of deliberate dependence, voluntary enslavement, and general disarray that is simply frightening.

Nomad? Not when you're ceaselessly wired, under 'round-the-clock surveillance!

"Hello Jacques, hello Elodie, hello Marcel, call me back!"

To be always reachable is no doubt the great fantasy of mobile subscribers – a fantasy that the invention of the portable certainly fulfills. Yet it is no less certain that this fulfillment makes it impossible to hear a call that comes not from others but from within, a call that you can only pick up in that vital silence when you are listening to your own inner voice.

And the Other. Do we really listen to this Other, who from now on can reach us anywhere we happen to be – from whom no distance can separate us? Do we hear a unique, irreplaceable specificity? The joy of the irruption of the Other's voice: a presence close to us, impalpable perhaps, but indubitable and at times overwhelming. Here, the voice – the grain of the voice – is apt to signify to us what will never happen again.

This intimate collapse through the grace of the beloved voice – this shudder – becomes an appalling wrench when the voice that so often assures us of continued love calls to say that it – love – is over. We swing from a state of grace to rejection. This communication, the final one – a full stop – which is a kind of death without the body being touched, reveals with cruel clarity the ambiguity of the telephone, the presence-absence which is its secret. Cocteau notes as a prelude to his play, *La Voix humaine* (1930), where the entire action is reduced to a woman speaking on the phone: "The actress should give the impression that she is bleeding, losing her blood, like a wounded animal, ending the act in a pool of blood." For the woman abandoned, whose tears often prevent her from going on, the moment when the man hangs up will be the ultimate moment of rupture. "I'm in pain, I'm in pain. This line is the last thing binding me to us." Whence the final cry: "Hurry up. Go on. Hang up! Hang up, now! I love you, I love you, I love you, I love you, I love you . . . *The receiver falls to the ground.*"

Though the voice intones its imminent vanishing, it is the reverse that happens, making the whole thing that much more painful – sensually, physically painful. It is the hallucinatory force of the man's presence that the woman still feels forever close. This ultimate communication, intended as a way of imposing absence, excites a frantic desire for presence, in all its impossibility. The telephone, "a most inept device for dealing with matters of the heart," according to Cocteau, is the perfect device for making you suffer and keeping you within the dependency of suffering by producing the simultaneous lure of a palpable proximity.

When Proust first gives Céleste Albaret a lesson in phoning, he begins by telling her: "There's no need to be frightened, Céleste. It's very simple. All you have to do is imagine you're talking to someone."

It's very simple, indeed, when you are reciting some impersonal message, automatically engaging in some banal exchange whose sole aim is to relay or obtain information. Simple, yes. "All you have to do is imagine you're talking to someone." But if you are not on autopilot, if you are not reciting a phrase learned by rote, if that someone means more to you than anyone else in the world, is it always so simple? Obviously not. For proof, if proof were needed, recall the passage in *À La Recherche* where the narrator engages in a telephone conversation with his grandmother. Through "the wondrous telephone fairy" (or, more concretely, with the aid of those then-indispensable intermediaries, the *Demoiselles* of the telephone exchange), the narrator, who is staying in Doncières, manages to be put in contact with the longed-for voice. But what he hears in that voice – "in that poor broken voice" whose weariness and great age he suddenly perceives – is a premonition of its disappearance. This loving voice, hoping to bring him presence and reassurance, indicates in a subtone its impending and ultimate absence. The narrator is seized with a terrible anguish, close enough, he feels, to what he will feel "the day you speak to those who can no longer reply." He immediately decides to return to Paris to relieve his anxiety, to ward off the phantom that springs solely from a voice – to snatch his grandmother from the grasp of the shades.

At the opposite extreme of such panic, when confronted by presence-absence (or by absence-presence as in Cocteau's *La Voix humaine*), the portable phone rings and resonates to reassure. This new extension that has grown into the palm of our hand repeats its message in all tones, through the intermediary of all possible interlocutors: *it's very simple.* It is not only my functioning that is very simple – even infantile – but what it allows: *communication.*

The mania for communication in the open air, in the public arena; the constant concern to reach and be reachable, in broad daylight, which is the enemy of phantoms and extinguishes the audible voice's undertone of loss as much as its dizzying presence, its deathly double, its abrupt desire – what could be more foreign to "the night full of apparitions to which our ears alone are open"?

"I'm at Muette Station, I don't know if I'll be coming home tonight . . ."

CHANTAL THOMAS IS A RESEARCHER AT THE CENTRE NATIONAL DE LA RECHERCHE SCIENTIFIQUE IN PARIS. SHE IS THE AUTHOR OF *MARQUIS DE SADE: L'OEIL DE LA LETTRE* (1978) AND *CASANOVA: UN VOYAGE LIBERTIN* (1985).

Centrale

In a central district of Beirut once close to the east/west demarcation line of the civil war (1975-1990) and abandoned until recently, stands Centrale, a restaurant and bar built in the reclaimed space of a 1920s residential structure. Although now under a preservation mandate, the area has lacked concerted public revitalization initiatives since the war ended. The result is a climate of private investment, largely based on entertainment businesses, with bars, restaurants, and movie theaters now appearing in large numbers.

To accommodate a restaurant in the battle-scarred house, architect Bernard Khoury removed all of the interior partitions and the second-story floor slab. In the process of clearing out the interior, the outer envelope of the house had to be reinforced with horizontal metal banding that embraced the façade. The resulting internal void, nine meters high, was achieved by simultaneously pouring structural concrete along the inside of the walls and bracing the space with ring beams. This process is visible in the final configuration of the structure, implying a perhaps unexpected reading of the reclaimed space. Further emphasizing the temporal dimension of the project and its position vis-à-vis the "historical value" of the building, Khoury chose not to replaster the sandstone façade, instead covering it with a metal mesh behind which the plaster continues to peel. The structure itself is protected by a waterproof membrane applied between the sandstone and the internal layer of concrete. The façade, then, is handled as a temporal register and invites reflection on the poetics of decay and preservation. It also asks, What does it mean to rebuild? To preserve? How much of the past do we erase?

Inside, the double volume of the now large hall contains a conference-style table – similar to a conference table for a general assembly – that seats 46 diners, all looking inward. The service staff is surrounded by and "trapped" within the table, but can communicate directly with the subterranean kitchen via a flight of stairs. Guests seated at the table are enveloped in an atmosphere of formality: imposing high-back chairs imitate the discreet enclosure of a secret assembly, while 46 pilot lamps – which resemble microphones – sharply

CENTRALE, A RESTAURANT IN A FOR-
MER HOUSE DAMAGED IN BEIRUT'S
CIVIL WAR. A NEW ENTRANCE ALSO
HOUSES AN ELEVATOR TO A ROOFTOP
BAR. PRECEDING AND OPPOSITE
PAGES: THE CRUMBLING PLASTER
FAÇADE IS REINFORCED WITH METAL
BANDING AND WIRE MESH. IMAGES
COURTESY OF BERNARD KHOURY.

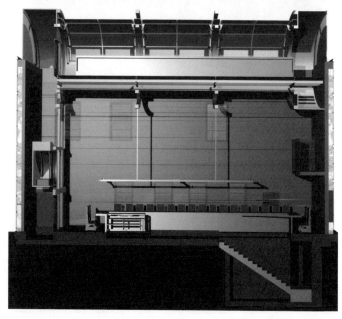

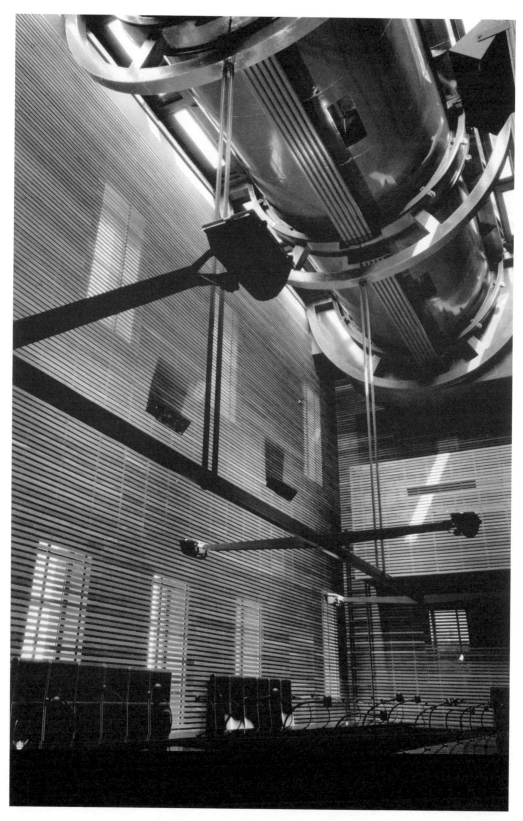

The walls of the two-story-high dining room are covered with wood lathe that runs over the windows as well, obscuring their residential character but still allowing light to penetrate the interior. The tubular machinery of the rooftop bar is exposed above the conference-like dining table that seats 46. Images courtesy of Bernard Khoury.

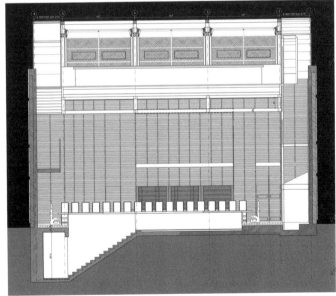

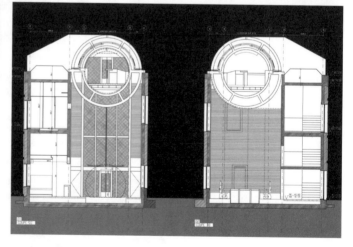

THE OPEN ROOFTOP BAR AT
CENTRALE, SEEN FROM WITHIN AND
WITHOUT. RIGHT: SECTIONS.

illuminate each plate. An enormous fixture suspended above the table provide ambient light. Adjacent to the large hall is an alternative to this monolithic arrangement: three separate "loggias," each able to accommodate six diners.

In a move that recalls the mechanism's of Khoury's earlier nightclub, B018 (*B-dix-huit*) – which resembled a piece of military machinery – at the top of Centrale, he placed a large circular section inscribed by four ring beams and containing a 17-meter-long bar. For Khoury, this metal tube is a symbolic merging of elemental geometry, the language of structure, and the project's program. One segment of the bar is vertically mobile, becoming an elevator that links the two levels. Two deep benches in the elevator cabin conform to the volume's unusual section. The bar's cylindrical envelope rotates in a track, allowing the roof to be opened like a window and giving views onto the various degrees of ruin and regeneration in contemporary Beirut. Seen from the outside, the bar appears as a luminous tube, beckoning patrons and perhaps protecting the previously endangered structure and its users from further mishap.

BERNARD KHOURY IS AN ARCHITECT
IN BEIRUT. HIS B018 APPEARED IN
ANY 24 IN 1999.

JULIE EISENBERG AND MIKE MENEGAZZI, TERRAZZO/TILE INSTALLATION IN "MASONRY VARIATIONS," AT THE BUILDING MUSEUM, OCTOBER 18, 2003 – APRIL 4, 2004. PHOTO COURTESY OF THE BUILDING MUSEUM.

The giant columns of the Building Museum in Washington, D. C., tend to diminish the effect of architectural installations. So it was a pleasant surprise to come across "Masonry Variations," curated by Stanley Tigerman and effectively installed in four gallery–sized rooms. His pairing of four architects with four masonry craftsmen produced elegant, thoughtful projects in stone, brick, terrazzo, and concrete, reflecting the post-postmodern-pastiche interest in materiality today and its capacity to achieve new effects. Chicago architect Jeanne Gang and stone carver Matthew Stokes Redabaugh constructed a stone curtain, in which increasingly thin pieces of stone were hung like puzzle pieces, one from the other, creating a tepeelike construction held in tension rather than compression. (The piece would later fail, but its initial construction was materially and structurally sublime.) Equally surprising, and satisfying for its twist on an old architectural idea, was Santa Monica architect Julie Eizenberg and terrazzo craftsman Mike Menegazzi's installation. An undulating floor of smooth black terrazzo rolls upward to become a wall, where rough-cut stone emerges from the cemented surface as if straining to return to its natural state. The material was used to exquisite effect, but the intriguing concept was the rolling floor/wall relationship, which reposed a quintessential architectural question: Which came first: the wall or the floor?– Cynthia Davidson

Giuliana Bruno

Architects of Time: Reel Images from Warhol To Tsai Ming-Liang

No more actors, no more story, no more sets, which is to say that in the perfect aesthetic illusion of reality there is no more cinema.
— André Bazin

A building, seen from a window. No actors, no story, no sets. A simple "location," a map of place. Still, yet moving in time. From night to daylight, architecture moves at the speed of the (every)day here. For eight hours, we watch this architectural *Empire* (1964) exist.

In Andy Warhol's famous but little-seen film, the skyscraper comes into being over the course of time, becoming an architecture of light. The effect is uncanny when the film is screened today, given the posthumous "reflections" cast by the World Trade Center and considering the shadows that such reflections have projected, sometimes literally, onto the architectural reconfiguration of Ground Zero. It seems even more uncanny now that a skyscraper has acquired the status of a lamp of memory by incarnating lights that are the ghosts of a building.

In Warhol's version of a building's form, made before this time, the life of the skyscraper becomes, in time, the very spirit of light. As we watch, the tectonics of building transforms into the architecture of light. The façade of the skyscraper molds into pure reflective matter. In this way, architecture and film are tangibly connected. The two mediums meet on the grounds of their shared light texture, mor-phing into each other. Both are rendered as surfaces, screens – materials prone to absorb and cast back light. In this *Empire* of architecture, the skin of the building actually turns into celluloid.

A tangible film of a building emerges from the compression of urban movement into the steady rhythm of geographical tempo. In this cinematic architectonics, sensing place is achieved through the observation of time passing and the feeling of light changing. Through this phenomenological construction of a filmic architecture, a meteorology is built:

STILLS FROM *EMPIRE* (1964) BY ANDY
WARHOL. 16 MM FILM, B/W, SILENT, 8
HOURS, 5 MINUTES. FROM TOP: REEL
1: JULY 25, 1964, AT APPROXIMATELY
8:13 PM; 8:24 PM; 8:30 PM; AND (OPPO-
SITE PAGE) 8:35 PM.

architecture becomes weather report. By following so closely
the passage of light between night and day, the film records
the building's atmospheric life – subtle changes in the air,
light particles, shifts in visibility, clouded visions, hazy con-
tours, blur. What finally unfolds in this moving portrait of the
Empire State Building is the actual rhythm of a site. The
film reveals the extent to which architecture is sensitive to
atmosphere. In fact, it makes architecture into pure atmosphere. Such is the real spirit of Warhol's "reel time." His cultural "climate" is the very *Empire* of atmosphere.

***

Now turn from a building to a face. It is time to watch
another microphysiognomy. Here is the head of a man. There
is no story here either. The man is acting out an ordinary
event. He is getting his *Haircut* (1963). A decent haircut cannot be cut short. No way to perform it in less than half an
hour. From different angles we watch, along with other by-
standers, this real cut with no reel cuts.

***

A man with a hat. This man acts out nothing more than
a domestic routine. The set is a simple daily action, which
includes a cat – no particular story. The man is just eating.
To *Eat* (1963) a mushroom can take a while. We watch and
ingest, "consuming" the film. An absorption of images, a
visual feast, cinema is an oral affair.

***

I *Kiss* (1963), you kiss, he kisses, she kisses, we kiss, you
kiss, they kiss. A serial of touching images. The oral action of
couples kissing is a sample of the many film portraits Warhol
made: recordings of people exhibiting daily behavior, enjoy-
ing leisure inactivity or pleasure time, from smoking a cigar

to having sex. They would hang out on camera until the rolls of film ran out. Shot in the manner of screen tests (a form the artist used literally, to record individual subjects' faces in close-up), Warhol's early films dwell in the atmosphere of life cycles as set in reel time.

***

No story, no sets. Just a body and a piece of furniture "couching" reel/real time. To *Sleep* (1963) well, one must be engaged in the act for at least six hours. To film a man sleeping, Warhol follows this everyday rule of atmospheric time. The sleeper is relentlessly explored across the course of time – repetitive, private time. Body parts take film parts. A breathing abdomen in close-up, a body lying, the cave of an armpit, the curve of a leg, a neck's suture, a dormant face – these take up the time of sleep.

WARHOL'S REEL TIME

"To show a man sleeping, is this a movie?" asked Jonas Mekas in 1972.[1] When even the avant-garde is puzzled enough to raise a question like this, the very nature of cinema is at stake. To ask if Warhol's *Sleep* is a movie is implicitly to pose André Bazin's question, "What is Cinema?" It means calling into question what the medium of film does, especially in relation to time, subjectivity, and space. Indeed, Warhol's films question the workings of cinema in these arenas. They are films that reidentify cinema in a manner that approaches the space of today's moving-image installations. They reconfigure a spectatorial protocol: the films yield to viewers walking around and talking in the theater; they encourage spacing out. Hyperrealist wanderings themselves, they tell us about the "zero degree" of film.

To approach the zero degree of cinema according to Warhol, a useful beginning is with Bazin. Bazin claimed that the invention of cinema arose from the techniques of observation of the 19th century, a time obsessed with the mechanical reproduction of the real. This obsession turned into early film's reel time and returned, transformed, at different moments of film history, eventually shaping the postwar aesthetic of neorealism.

Without the teleological bent, the outlines of Warhol's cinematic opus can be read as a movement from "primitive cinema" to Hollywood's modes of representation, for his film work retraces the very course of cinema's history.[2] Reproductive, as was his art work, it is an actual remake of film history. Warhol began by shooting silent black-and-white films – remade silent cinema – and then moved

1. Jonas Mekas, *Movie Journal: The Rise of a New American Cinema, 1959–1971* (New York: Collier, 1972), 109. On the relation of Warhol to the avant-garde, see also P. Adams Sitney, *Visionary Film: The American Avant-Garde 1943–1978* (Oxford: Oxford University Press, 1974); Annette Michelson, "'Where is Your Rupture?': Mass Culture and the Gesamtkunstwerk," *October* 56 (Spring 1991): 42–63; and Colin MacCabe, Mark Francis, and Peter Wollen, eds., *Who is Andy Warhol?* (London: British Film Institute, 1997).
2. See Gregory Battcock, "Four Films by Andy Warhol," in *Andy Warhol Film Factory*, ed. Michael O'Pray (London: British Film Institute, 1989), a useful collection of essays on Warhol's cinema.
3. On this topic, see Stephen Koch, *Stargazer: Andy Warhol's World and His Films* (New York: Praeger, 1973).
4. For a postmodern reading emphasizing "corporeal stupidity," see Steven Shaviro, "Warhol's Bodies," in *The Cinematic Body* (Minneapolis: University of Minnesota Press, 1993).
5. André Bazin, *What is Cinema?*, v. 2, ed. and trans. Hugh Gray (Los Angeles: University of California Press, 1971), 55.
6. Andy Warhol's statement is cited in Peter Gidal, "Warhol – Part One of an Analysis of the Films of Andy Warhol," *Films and Filming* 7 (April 1971): 27. For a more recent treatment of Warhol in the context of the aesthetic of boredom, see Patrice Petro, "After Shock/Between Boredom and History," in *Fugitive Images*, ed. Patrice Petro (Bloomington: Indiana University Press, 1995).

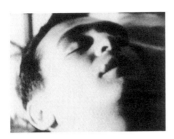

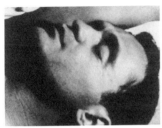

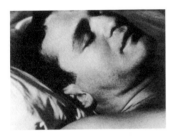

STILLS FROM *SLEEP* (1963) BY ANDY
WARHOL. 16 MM FILM, B/W, SILENT, 5
HOURS 21 MINUTES. JOHN GIORNO
PICTURED IN TAKES FROM REELS 1, 2,
4 AND 5. © 2004 THE ANDY WARHOL
MUSEUM, PITTSBURGH, A MUSEUM OF
THE CARNEGIE INSTITUTE.

toward stargazing.[3] The reinvention of the language of motion pictures in his early films reproduces early cinema's interest in daily life. Even literally: *Kiss*, Warhol's first released film, treats the subject and even bears the same title of an 1896 Edison short.

Although often engaging sexuality, even when the object is simply a skyscraper occupying erect space, Warhol's peeking at the real is not really a form of voyeurism. His films do "take a look," and certainly corporeally "expose."[4] The pleasure they offer, however, does not involve peeking at unaware subjects but rather watching and experiencing diffraction. Warhol's early films provide the pleasure of peeking into the gap – and exhibiting the suture – between the real and the reel, between real time and reel time. Shot at twenty-four frames per second and projected at sixteen (the speed of silent film), these films are not a matter-of-fact reproduction of the real. They are cinematic "meditations" on real matters. Real performances, they look at how reality itself matters.

It is for this reason that Bazin's writings on neorealism, an extract from which is offered at the opening of this inquiry, become particularly pertinent in examining Warhol's reel/real time and space. Although Bazin was not writing about *Empire* – a vertical story of nothing but "light" urban architectures – he defined the zero degree of cinema by thinking architecturally. Writing about *The Bicycle Thief* (1949), a film shot on location in an urban setting, he recognized it as nothing but "the story of a walk through Rome."[5] In this way, Bazin arrived at defining an architectonics of location as the reel time of space.

Following this logic of urban reelism, the experimental film *Empire* paradoxically turns out to be one of the most realistic films ever made. Its realism abides in the space of its duration, in the sustained exploration of an architectural atmosphere. It resides in the "exhibition" of nothing but the span of architectural time and the time of architectural space. In this rhythmic observational sense, this is, indeed, an "atmosphere" film.

As Warhol once said: "When you just sit and look out the window, that's enjoyable. It takes up time. . . If you're not looking out of a window, you're sitting in a shop looking at the street. My films are just a way of taking up time."[6] This statement, among others, gives us room to read Warhol's early cinema as exhibiting an aesthetic of boredom. Indeed, Warhol can be seen as practicing a type of boredom theory and, in such a way, translating into cinema an aspect of the discourse of modernity – a discourse in which boredom abides alongside distraction and shock. But if Warhol's work, broadly understood, engages boredom, it does so in a complex way – as a tempo in the larger context of an exploration of modern forms of subjectivity. Modernity's exploration involved a spatialization – the journey through time. Picturing the body's temporality and architectural duration, Warhol's film work expanded a modern(ist) filmic zone. His films signaled the rise of a late-modernist aesthetics, characterized in the cinema by a preoccupation with duration.

Duration, a Modern Geology

Pausing to grasp this movement of atmospheric duration, let us reread Warhol's statement – "My films are just a way of *taking up time*" – and think again of *Empire*. You sit and look out the window. That's enjoyable. If you are not looking out the window, you are sitting at street level, looking at the street. Warhol's urban take recalls an urban tale, a passage in Henri Lefebvre's *Writings on Cities*, in which, to introduce the notion of "rhythmanalysis," the author tells himself: "I must write: 'Seen from my windows overlooking a big intersection in Paris, therefore onto the street.'"[7]

7. Henri Lefebvre, *Writings on Cities*, ed. and trans. Eleonore Kofman and Elizabeth Lebas (Cambridge: Blackwell, 1996), 219.

As in Lefebvre's own rhythmanalysis, a film like *Empire* engages the production of daily urban rhythms. It opens a filmic window onto architectural space and its existence in time. Filmically exploring architectural duration, alongside the time of sleeping, eating, kissing, or getting a haircut, Warhol's early cinema touches on the very mechanism of the time and space of the everyday. It furthermore engages the practice of everyday life and its production of space. Taking on the time of sex, food, or architecture, Warhol's films take up a bodily landscape. Here, the atmosphere of dailiness is a space of incorporation.

This absorption of images involves a time that is spatialized. The eight hours of *Empire* render the time of architecture as the space of history. A building is "planted" in a city. It is immobile, yet in the course of a day it becomes a vehicle for many motions. It holds the motion of time and the passing of people. Day after day, a building lives this way, atmospherically. As darkness turns to light, the building, withstanding time, stands there. As times go by, it is inhabited, eroded, traversed, negotiated, navigated.

Like the sea, architecture transports. And like an ocean, it inhabits duration. It abides the time of history that modern historians interested in space, such as Fernand Braudel, call the *longue durée*. Duration – the time span that was once proper to geology and a property of landscape – now transfers to architecture. The architectural landscape is the geology of modern life. The depth of the terrain reveals strata of urban planning and layers of ruin. The cityscape is our horizon line. Skyscrapers are the mountains of cities. Watching them *be*, simply exist, in space and time, as in Warhol's *Empire*, is to experience the expanse of geological time – an earthly lingering.

As we look at *Empire* and think of architecture as the place where bodies *Sleep*, we approach the ticking of biological clocks. This cinema lets us meditate on the time of the body. It gets us close to interior time. Slow motion finally reveals an interior landscape. This landscape emerges, right in the midst of New York City, if one just sits (in a movie theater) and watches (a building), letting one's self be transported by the atmosphere of either.

THE ATMOSPHERE OF *TEMPS MORT*

Unlike early modernism, which was more interested in speed, velocity, and acceleration, the late modernism that emerged in the postwar period conceived of modernity as inhabiting different, extended temporal zones, and it set out to explore this new shape of modern times. Broadening, expanding, fragmenting, layering, exploring, rethinking time marked a new international filmic movement. As an architectonics of duration, Warhol's early cinema was in tune with its time and joined with filmmaking practices involved, in different ways, in developing the rhythm of late modern(ist) cinematics.

Among the most prominent artists to experiment with these practices – at the time when Warhol was creating *Empire* and *Sleep* – was Michelangelo Antonioni, the architectural filmmaker who was articulating modernist (filmic) space by dwelling on the architectonics of time. In his modernist view, reel time became something other than the abridged, compressed, sped-up time of conventional cinema. His cinema privileged description over plot, fashioning a filmic *nouveau roman*. It was an aesthetic of *temps mort*, absorbed in framing and mapping (interior) landscapes and drawn to the time of nonaction, a time when actors stop acting and space tells its story. Journeying in postdiegesis space – that is, dwelling on the time after characters have left the scene, lingering on that space, navigating the leftovers of time, exploring the slow motion of an architectural everyday – Antonioni, in a way, joined in Warhol's interest in the profilmic, reaching for a zero degree of cinema.

The redesign of reel/real time in the modernist cinema

87

that emerged around Warhol opened the road to a new geography, one which included new maps of gender space. As modernist aesthetics peered at new temporalities and the time of everyday life, there arose a questioning of the gendered realm of lived space and lived time. Chantal Akerman's exquisitely minimalist long take, in particular, began calling modern(ist) duration to (real) task. Repetition, private time, the unfolding of ordinary temporalities, the rhythm of the everyday, the time when seemingly nothing goes on – all this has been radically called into question as a corporeal texture of woman's time in Akerman's work.

Today, such modern architectural ruminations are re-emerging in a series of urban images from the East. Perhaps the most direct heir of the architectonics of duration is the Malaysian-born, Taiwan-based filmmaker Tsai Ming-Liang. He, too, works in "reel" time as he reengages Akerman's early filmic strategies and picks up exactly where Antonioni left off. There is a relevant formal relation between Akerman's "domestic" films and Tsai's interiors, and both are rigorous filmmakers whose style is relentlessly challenging. They use contemplative compositions characterized by long takes, which are fixed.

Like Akerman and Antonioni, Tsai dwells in the space of observation with a resolute fixation on staying and lingering within the frame. Working slowly, from inside out, Tsai's films take time to make incisive portraits of the urban condition and its affective discontents, with a minimalist architectural framing that exposes the very architecture of time. As in Antonioni's own rendering of urban disquiet and amorous malaise, the camera stays with a space for a long period, as if to draw us in and absorb us, enveloping us within a frame that is a frame of mind. This type of cinema resides inside a mental space, which is an architecture of interiors. In fact, it shows that the rhythm of the city coincides with that of a person's own internal clock. Ultimately, the setting here is the internal rhythm of urban life, for the city is seen through an inner eye. This cinema represents place, minimally, as a subjective space, a mental state – an atmosphere.

An empty apartment. A bed. A bath tub. There is little else here, but a story develops out of this void. The apartment is for sale. This lifeless space becomes casually inhabited by three lonely people: a real-estate agent, her accidental lover, and someone who steals the key to the place to kill himself there quietly. No one moves into the empty apartment, but all use it as a way to be with themselves or attempt an encounter. In shot after shot, we watch this empty place simply *be*, observe it being transformed, and see it failing to become the catalyst for a relational connection. There is irony in the film and its title, *Vive L'Amour* (1994), for love cannot be found anywhere near the place. Finally exiting the apartment, without resolution, we walk with the real-estate agent to a city park. There she sits, for a long time, crying. After a while she stops weeping. But then she cries some more. In this memorable sequence of internal rain, which turns sadness into smile, the camera, as always, simply watches, at once impassive and compassionate, until the end.

In this architectonics of time we are neither voyeurs nor detectives who spy on characters. By virtue of the camera position, which refuses to move with the characters and rolls independently, remaining steady in time, we cannot pry. We are simply there. Witnesses, we are made to exist in the space. We are asked to stay overtime. This "being there" enables us to make a psychic leap and go beyond mere attendance toward a more intimate involvement. Reaching for a closer spectatorial position, we can stay there to take part in a scene, becoming participants. As an affective atmosphere unfolds in slow time-space, we can let ourselves slide in. We can take in what is in the air and partake in a mood. In this moody way, affects turn around. We become mourners, lovers, eaters, sleepers.

Another person is sitting at a table, eating. A daily routine. No particular story. It takes him a while to eat. As we watch, we ingest as well. When the man dies, we continue to sit at the table with his wife and son, who try to digest this death. Time is the only way to deal with "passing." Time passing, in fact, becomes the very question in Tsai's *What Time Is It There?* (2001). While the mother awaits the reincarnation of her husband's soul, the son finds a different temporal strategy to deal with matters of life and death.

A seller of cheap watches on a skyway in Taipei, he becomes obsessed with time. A casual meeting with a young woman who buys his watch en route to Paris sets off in him the wish to live differently – in her time. Perhaps in an attempt to get closer to her, he proceeds to change the time of every clock he sells and encounters in the city of Taipei, adjusting them to Paris time. As he travels the city to change the time, moving from the clock atop a skyscraper down into the computerized time that runs the city's subway, Taipei turns into Paris. Meanwhile, she melancholically travels *la ville lumière*. The film proceeds in parallel montage. The two never meet or cross paths again. They simply become connected in this virtual time zone.

SCENES FROM *THE SKYWALK IS GONE* (2001) BY TSAI MING-LIAN.. COURTESY OF THE TAPEI CULTURAL CENTER, NEW YORK.

In the end, everyone in this film is bound to inhabit his or her own time, while dreaming of sharing it. Such is the time of urban loneliness, which is given room here: the time one spends with oneself; the time of retreat, withdrawal, seclusion, or hibernation; the time of nonaction. A *temps mort*. It is the leftovers of time, recaptured to feed the self. Morsels of time extended, even wasted, squandered, dissipated, used up. The time of luxuriating in time. The time of reflection, stolen away from pressure. That private time, reclaimed from functionality. The place where so often fears, anxiety, melancholia, and desire settle in. In other words, inner time.

In Tsai's interior films we watch characters carry out elaborate private rituals. Everything one does with oneself in one's own time is the real focus of Tsai's cinema. This includes the display of bodily functions, sleeping or being unable to sleep, finding a way to take a leak without having to walk to the bathroom. All matters of eating, sleeping, kissing unravel in reel time here, and often in the same place.

In fact, in an architectural ritual, Tsai often uses the same apartment as his location for different films, and thus these daily actions are positioned for us in a home that literally becomes familiar. In most of his films he also uses the same nonprofessional actor, Lee Kang-Sheng, whom he discovered in a video arcade and who inhabits, not acts, his characters. Hence mother, father, son, and the apartment (fish tank included) travel from film to film, enabling us to follow a private routine and take part in a private life that is always architecturally bound. Emotions are given a real place here. The stories are written on the walls of the apartment. The films build on the feeling of the place. We get to know and recognize the atmosphere. We sense the mood changing. It breathes out from the walls and leaks down through the pipes.

In fact, it all starts with a leak. There is a gaping *Hole* (1998), and for Tsai this is a sensational subject for a movie. As the title suggests, here we have a film about a void: nothing but a hole; the hole is it. The film dwells in hollow space, and in this way it tackles a very architectural issue. It explores architecture's generative void. This is a cinema that dares to look at architecture at its zero degree and builds stories out of its bare bone.

The leak sets the film in motion. It always rains in Tsai's films, whether from the inside or the outside. A corporeal rain is present in the seepage of our plumbing or in our tears. As the filmmaker said, "Water is like love, we all need it but

8. From a roundtable discussion with the
author, at the Harvard Film Archive,
Harvard University, 7 October 2003.
9. For a more extended treatment of
filmic architecture and Sugimoto's own
architectures, see Giuliana Bruno, *Atlas
of Emotion: Journeys in Art, Architecture,
and Film* (London and New York: Verso,
2002).
10. See Norman Bryson, "Hiroshi
Sugimoto's Metabolic Photography,"
Parkett 46 (1996): 120–23.

do not know what to do with it."[8] As in real life, in this reel
life things always leak. Holes are always there. One can
never really fill them in and perhaps should not even try, for
one never knows what is actually hidden in a hole.

Here, the hole works its magic. Left by a plumber who
has tried to fix a leak in the apartment after an interminable
rain, the hole becomes the character of the film. This hole,
an empty space, becomes filled with wonderful stories. It
also becomes pregnant with gags. Tsai uses reel time the way
Jacques Tati did in his urban critiques and architectural
mediations. As in "Tativille," the slow, silent observation of
architectural space enables us to see the ironies of life. Here,
the hole enables characters to overcome the emptiness of
loneliness. It creates a connection between the inhabitants
of two apartments, above and below. The leak-turned-hole
takes up room and makes room. The hollow becomes an
actual space. There is even holiness to this hole. A hole is,
after all, literally and metaphorically many things: crater,
cavity, pit, shaft, pocket, interval, intermission, indentation.
In the end, it can even turn into a real opening.

ARCHITECTURE AND FILM AT GROUND ZERO

What emerges from this attachment to the space of nothingness and void is a cinema that is pure spatial meditation – a
cinema of atmospheric moods. We can see how this relates to
Empire, with its own architectural unfolding in time. In a
way, speaking of *Empire* is a way to engage the wide-ranging
development of a filmic-architectural minimalism of atmosphere: no acting, but space acting out; no sets, but locations
unraveling in reel time. Real stories of place. This is the
ground zero of filmic architectures. In this aesthetic zone, as
we have traversed it in time, the zero degree of cinema is the
zero degree of architecture.

To dwell in this zero degree exposes a transition that
reveals the moment of film's own emergence and extinction.
In this respect, watching *Empire* is a spectatorial experience
that engages film space in the transient manner of Hiroshi
Sugimoto's film *Theaters* – pictures that render film as "light"
architecture.[9] These pictures are conceived at the crossroads
between modernity's extended temporality and a Buddhist
sense of time.[10] In his photographic journey, Sugimoto also
travels in a phenomenological, atmospheric terrain.

Sugimoto achieves duration by adjusting the exposure
time of his photographs to the length of a feature film that is
projected in the theater he is depicting. The effect is that the
film itself disappears from view, leaving only the image of a

white film screen. But something else becomes visible: the architecture of cinema is exposed. Neither shown nor show, the filmic text ends up shaping a picturing of cinema. A blaze of light emerges from the screen, casting an eye on the "interior" space of the theater. As pure screen, cinema shows its atmospheric texture and durational substance. This "reel" time constructs film's real visual space – a spatialized time. No more actors, no more stories, no more sets, no more cinema. The zero degree of cinema is the space of movie-going – a geography that takes place in the architecture of the movie "house." Cinema is a house: a home of voyages, an architecture of the interior; it is a map of shifting atmospheres.

Representing cinema at the moment of generative extinction, Sugimoto casts it as a morbid space and links it to other modern heterotopias of this kind. On the map of modernity's time zone, Sugimoto's sea of film images adjoins his images of wax museums and the natural-history view of his dioramas. Looking at his photographic series as interconnected, the geological time of history is exposed. Moving with times of *longue durée*, Sugimoto's series render the geography through which corporeal stories are told – a transient, floating world of ruination. This is a meditation on modernity and its ruins, a place of "accelerated decrepitude," as *Blade Runner* describes it. In such a way, Sugimoto's morbid physicality and duration engage modernity's speed. Incorporating the very speed of cinema in a rendering of ruination – indeed, making it the very "exposure" of such a state – Sugimoto's architectonics join Warhol's atmospheric "reel film" of *Empire* on the very space of modern representation and its ruins.

East Meets West

What is at stake in charting these meditative relations is the construction of a genealogy, built around the *Empire* of atmosphere. Speaking of Warhol's reel time, and then considering a series of "still lives" that touches on Akerman, Antonioni, Tati, Tsai Ming-Liang, and Sugimoto, means drafting a set of spatio-temporal connections on the late modern(ist) map rather than proposing a series of influences. Warhol is the preface, for he was a symptom – the expression of a cultural movement, a figure able to cathect the cultural energy, or atmosphere, of a time.

Just as Warhol was a master of appropriation, so in turn he has been appropriated, even indirectly. His strategies of taking up time are transposed into other film work and even transferred into other visual forms. Warhol's *Sleep* is a case in point, for it has been reawakened in different fashions. The time of *Sleep* has reappeared in an aesthetic of duration in different forms. If the extended duration of Warhol's early cinema is read as an aesthetic weightlessness, and his minimized sensory output is perceived as the creation of a spectatorial bliss or trance, then Buddhist-informed returns can be expected.[11] "Sleepers," however transformed, have imaginatively returned in this way, from the East, in the work of video artist Bill Viola. The form of video installation – a spatio-visual technology of present duration – has given Viola the opportunity to restage the present tense of *Sleep*. Warhol's "time exposed" becomes Viola's *The Sleep of Reason* (1988). *The Sleepers* (1992) now lie in barrels of steel filled with water; they repose in monitors, casting a bluish light that illuminates space. While electronic signboards broadcast news reports outside, we step into an entryway, thirty years later, and again "face" a Warholian sleeper, featured in large projection, resting in a dark room permeated only by the silence of sleeping noises. In this video passage to inner life, *Sleep* becomes a *Threshold* (1992).

11. An interpretation offered by David James in his *Allegories of Cinema: American Film in the Sixties* (Princeton: Princeton University Press, 1989), 65.

THE ARCHITECTURE OF TIME

Many passages of time have taken place in a history of late-modernist moving images. This history has not only exposed the architecture of time but especially the idea that architecture itself is a matter of time, and not simply of space. Architecture is the actual dwelling of temporality, its very home. Along these lines, Warhol's *Sleep* and *Empire* can be seen as part of a cultural movement that engages the urban-filmic architecture of (private) time. With these films, Warhol created a home for time travelers who are city wanderers, and even gave it a new architectural form. The durational architecture of *Empire* was to have a correlate in a new kind of urban movie theater. To enhance the atmosphere of the film, Warhol dreamed up the construction of a specific movie "house." *Empire* was to be shown in a space where spectators could lie down on the floor and watch the light architecture of the building unroll on the ceiling. This artist changed the frontal directional frame of cinema in favor of a different architecture for film. This ceiling-screen was to hold the temporal, unfolding architectonics of everyday life. With this *Empire* of atmosphere, Warhol anticipated recent trends in art installation, foreseeing even the shape that the projection of moving images has taken today. In the contemporary art installation, architectures of light are often projected on walls and ceilings of rooms, and even on the surfaces of buildings, in endless loops, with the effect of enhancing the very geological time of architecture. In a history of longue durée, on moving screens, moving images have thus come to "architect" the very mood of inner life – a landscape of temps mort, a geology of passage.

Time To Let It Be

In many ways, the sixties and seventies have returned – have come back into fashion. Warhol, master of all trends, guides the reconsideration of an era. Retrospectives continually resurface on the cultural horizon. On such occasions, one hopes that remembering a trend of the sixties may become a real reawakening. Indeed, the sixties modernist aesthetic was, among other things, a political trend. It was a radical refashioning of a politics of time. In an era of reality bytes, a time of pressure and managerial efficiency where speed and simultaneity do not even allow for accelerated decrepitude, a time when the taylorization of creativity is biting us up and beating us down, Warhol's early films yet again have something creative to say. They are there to remind us of an important aspect of modernity and modernist aesthetics: a radical temporal refashioning of subjectivity. A politics of time means giving space to time. Make room. Look out the window. Look onto the street. Space out. Watch a building be. Take the time to eat your lunch. Take up time. Get a hair cut. Take your time. Massage your soul. Sleep. Dream something up. Revel in this mood. Get lost in the empire of atmosphere. As in the unconscious, something always happens when nothing does.

Giuliana Bruno is professor of visual and environmental studies at Harvard University and author of *Atlas of Emotion: Journeys in Art, Architecture, and Film*, which received the Krasna Krausz Award for "the best book in the moving image world" this year.

Julie Rose
Translated from the French
by the Interviewer

Lunch at La Coupole With Paul Virilio

We meet for lunch at La Coupole. Paul Virilio is already seated by the time I have gotten across Boulevard Montparnasse in a freezing winter squall. He's inside on the left – he's always on the left – as I face the cavernous well of the restaurant, built as a palace of modern living in 1927 and still going strong. Today he's at the first table, perched on the banquette that runs the length of the wall. I sit down opposite him, but I am in the way of the waiters serving hardier patrons on the enclosed *terrasse,* so I quickly move to the padded place next to Paul on the banquette, and our *tête-à-tête* takes place *côte-à-côte*. We both order oysters, six *fines de claire* each, and when the plate arrives, Paul butters tiny slices of black bread for both of us. The oysters are sumptuous, strong, and briny, true *huîtres de l'océan*. Paul then has the steak tartare frites while I tuck in to the choucroute. It is a classic French meal. Little has changed here, despite changes of ownership and a notion among die-hard aficionados of La Coupole's American Bar that the place has degenerated into a mere *cantine de luxe*. It's simply indestructible. Paul polishes off his meal, except for the frites I pinch, and I get through most of the choucroute, leaving the end of a smoked pork sausage and a small pile of chou, as Paul keeps saying I don't have to eat it all. The "interview" doesn't begin until we've finished, and then it's more like a private public performance in this giant opera house of Paris chatter and clattering cutlery. Virilio's strong, clear voice is more than a match for the ambient noise, but the following has necessarily been edited due to the limits of a less cavernous space.

Julie Rose: *So, Paul, let's start with the war in Iraq.*

Paul Virilio: Are you sure it's working [he gestures toward the recorder]? Yes? Right. The war. The coalition war of prevention in Iraq was, what is now being acknowledged, a senseless war, as Jeffrey Record of the U.S. [Air Force's Air] War College claims. It's a war of distraction, it is not a war of necessity. This is exactly what I've been saying in the many interviews I've done for the past year apropos the war in Iraq. The first war in Iraq – which led to my book, *Desert*

Screen – was inevitable: one country invaded another country, so no problem. We were within a Clausewitzian perspective on war: there is a territory, there are states, there is an invasion, and so on. This war in Iraq, however, has been a distraction from the war against terrorism. Terrorism declared war on the world with the World Trade Center attack. On that score, I'm in complete agreement with the Pentagon and with American policy. But just as the war in Afghanistan was necessary – that nest of terrorists had to be cleaned out, and it went back, moreover, to the war against the Soviets in Afghanistan – Bush's invasion of Iraq was a serious strategic mistake.

I'm not kidding; I've got with me here [takes out a newspaper clipping] the text of an article by Jeffrey Record, which has just been published in the review of the [U.S. Army] War College [Strategic Studies Institute].[1] He says exactly what I've been saying: the war against terrorism is not a war in the sense Carl von Clausewitz meant. Why? Because it is not a political war in the sense of a nation invading another nation, in the sense of a state, which has borders, which has rules, which declares war, and which has armies that do battle. We are looking at an accidental war. We are not looking at a substantial war of the kind Clausewitz describes. We are looking at an accidental war, that is, one that can't be won. Why? Because you can't win a war when you don't know the enemy. It's not just me saying that. It's the facts. Whether we like it or not, since 2001 we've been in a situation of strategic chaos. We have to find a way of counteracting the conflict, which is intrinsically different from the riposte of local war or of global war, which, after all, the Americans can launch because they are effectively superpowerful.

For me, Iraq is a war that has been not only an error but a mistake, which is worse for a general. Let me remind you that I was a staff officer and I know the military milieu. Let me also remind you that my books are taught in the American military academies. So I'm speaking as a professional on military matters. I'm not in the army but I am a child of war, a "war baby." I know all about war. As I said in *The Insecurity of the Territory*, war has been my father and my mother. I'm not speaking as someone who has some professional skill recognized by a diploma. My final rank was as *sergent-chef* – I don't know how you say that in English – you know, the three chevrons . . .

1. To read Dr. Jeffrey Record's complete essay, "Bounding the Global War on Terrorism," go to: www.carlisle.army.mil/ssi/pubs/2003/bounding/bounding.htm to download an Acrobat file of the text.

AUTHOR, ARCHITECT, AND TEACHER
PAUL VIRILIO OUTSIDE LA COUPOLE,
JANUARY 14, 2004. PHOTO: JULIE ROSE.

JR: *Master sergeant, I think.*

PV: So I'm not a general, nor am I a captain, but you see what I'm saying. The other aspect is the disaster of the information war – the fact that the Americans are the masters of information, via CNN, via the Internet, via the power of the American media. On that score, we've seen to what extent the whole thing was risible. People suddenly understood that this was war as spectacle, a war made for television – with the statue of Saddam Hussein being knocked over live, with George Bush landing on the *Abraham Lincoln* and announcing the end of the war. Since the end of the war, there have been 250 deaths [as of mid-January] and we're still counting. We are looking at a war that is not only catastrophic from a strategic point of view, senseless, but at a war that is merely distracting us from the real threat of the terrorist war, including weapons of mass destruction – and I don't mean those that they haven't found in Iraq. I'm talking about those that can be used more simply, at the level of a dirty bomb – which will happen in-ev-it-ab-ly one day or the next – in America, in Asia, in France, anywhere at all. Here we are faced with an issue that goes beyond Clausewitz. You know, Clausewitz was the great Prussian philosopher of war who inspired strategy, you could say, throughout the 19th and 20th centuries. Clausewitz is interesting because he understood that war was the continuation of politics by other means. Well, now we are looking at an innovation in strategy. We are outside the frame of war. This is a colossal event: the political form of war has collapsed into something like a sort of international civil war. It was Hannah Arendt who said we were heading for a worldwide civil war. This is a war of religion – since there is an Islamic dimension behind it – a war of religion, a war without enemies, without states, without armies, without flags, and sometimes even without anyone claiming responsibility – the most incredible thing about the WTC attack is that no one has claimed responsibility for it.

JR: *Obviously, you don't think it's Bin Laden.*

PV: It's not Bin Laden. So we are faced with an unheard-of situation – that's why I've been talking about an accidental war rather than a substantial war in the Aristotelian sense. Six months after the "end" of the war, we are faced with political chaos that can't be put right, and that is clearly going to lead to a whole string of terrorist attacks. It's already provoked the failure of peace in the Middle East, meaning Jerusalem, between the Palestinians and the Israelis. You could be forgiven for thinking that once the Americans won the war in Iraq, according to Bush W, they would then have the opportunity to influence Sharon, to reach a negotiated and political solution. I am for the state of Israel, you know. I'm not anti-Israeli – not at all.

JR: *Neither am I.*

PV: Good, good, we agree. Well, we can now see that the failure in Iraq has lead to the failure in Israel. In Israel they are in the middle of shutting themselves in behind a wall, which is absolutely crazy. Insane! Why is it insane? Because on the military plane, Israel's strength is what? Its strike force! When you overlap with the Palestinian settlements, your hands are tied. You can't use the atomic bomb when you are right on top of the enemy. What constitutes Israel's strength is that it has atomic power and a very strong armored division of the army. And all that is rendered useless. Useless! That's what I tell my Jewish friends, if they're Zionists. I tell them, you are mad! Don't you see you're about to shoot yourselves in the foot? You'll be locked in, and then how are you going to defend yourselves? Twenty-seven Israeli pilots wrote to their command saying exactly that.

You can see I'm getting carried away, but it's because it's so obvious. I'm not talking politics; I'm talking strategy. To be powerful, you need a field in which to deploy an army; to send in the armor, you need space, the Sinai . . .

JR: *And you need an exit plan.*

PV: An exit plan. When you shut yourself in, you are left with the police. Nothing but the police. And police mean civil war, right? You cannot win a civil war. Everybody loses if it's a civil war or a religious war. I live in La Rochelle. There were 25,000 Protestants living in La Rochelle when Richelieu laid siege to it in 1628: 20,000 of them died, only 5,000 survived. So don't talk to me about all that.

Sharon is not pursuing politics by other means. Neither is Arafat. Neither is Bush. So we are looking at a situation that is absurd. The worst possible. The most alarming. They're locking themselves in, sealing themselves off. You know what the situation at this point in time in the Middle East resembles? It resembles what you do when you want to kill your cat: you stuff it in a sack, you tie the sack, and you whack it. And that is sick. That is what the Middle East is like. I know nothing about the East, but it is not worthy of the intelligence of the West, which goes back to Machiavelli, to Clausewitz, and which is full of intelligent people who know when it's time to stop the fighting, when the war's gone on long enough, and to take a break, to observe a truce, the Truce of God; to say, let's stop. We're the strongest but let's stop and shake hands because it's gone too far. I say, I hate you, but I'm obliged to come to some agreement with you – I'm obliged to because it's all too stupid for words. That's what we've lost.

JR: *You say that Iraq is an accidental war. It's also been a war of accidents, an incredible number of accidents – Coalition members shooting each other down, an incredible number of helicopters falling out of the sky.*

PV: That's all there has been. I said in *Strategy of Deception* that we're heading for an accidental war, and I talked about the information bomb. Lots of people were shocked by the title, which is ridiculous. I've got a quote about this in the book [*La Ville panique* – Panic City – published by Galilée in January 2004]. There's a whole thing about it on the Internet. The moment the world is globalized, the moment it's interconnected, the moment it's live in real time – as far as stock exchange quotes go, as far as international trade goes, as far as information goes – when that information is *live*, the situation is no longer a democracy of opinion. It becomes a democracy of emotion; that is, thanks to television, the possibility of synchronizing what people feel on a planetary scale – which is what happened with the moon landing in '69 and what happened with the WTC – the whole world feels the same emotion at the same time. This is tele-evangelism. It's postpolitical. The possibility of synchronizing emotion is a new strategic phenomenon. Totally novel. It is used to manipulate opinion. We are looking at a new form of aggression. The situation with the information war has altered relations with the police and has undermined democracy.

Democracy used to be representative. Men and women voted for each other in what I'd call representative democracy; it worked through the vote. Thanks to the press, the news sheets, and the radio, because radio was different, we stumbled into a democracy of opinion, which was already no longer representative. Why? Because opinion can be individual whereas representation is collective. Direct democracy in Swiss cantons, for instance, entails presenting the subject, which people then go home and discuss together, and two weeks later they come out and vote – *la votation*. There is opinion, but it's collective because there is a pause, a lapse of time. The moment democracy becomes democracy of opinion, it votes individually. How many families do you see where the wife votes against the husband, systematically? To say nothing of the children – as in May '68, which turned the family on its head. Now, "democracy of emotion," in quotation marks, means religion. It's tele-evangelism. It's Billy Graham. Alleluya Aheueuh... Inshalam! Right? It's all the same. Billy Graham, Inshalam. It's all the same! It's Mecca. And so, here, we tumble into the abyss of democracy.

Democracy means time to reflect in common. In representative democracy, opinion is formed in common. In democracy of opinion, it becomes individual, it becomes sectarian, it's atomized. In synchronic democracy, we enter what I call in *La Ville panique* "mass individualism." Ancient societies were about mass collectivism. Now we have entered into mass individualism, we are a conditioned society. We are no longer a reflective society, but a society of conditioned reflexes.

JR: *You mean we buy the same things, wear the same things . . .*

PV: We can see to what extent the war in Iraq has used all the tricks picked up from marketing and advertising propaganda, There used to be political propaganda, as we saw with Nazism and communism. Now we have a form of advertising propaganda, and that's inspired the war in Iraq. All you have to do is look at the control of the American media by the Pentagon and the White House. It's unbelievable!

JR: *No one seems to be too worried about it.*

PV: It's new. The only people to redeem the situation have been actors – like Susan Sarandon – the Hollywood crew. What we've seen is an America not so much harking back to the McCarthy era but suddenly catapulted forward into unabashed conformism. And that is just not American. It's not the America I love. On the one hand, we have imperialist America, which we're all wary of, and on the other, this conformist America, which I've never seen before. You know, I'm much more successful in the United States than in

Europe – even though I've criticized America pretty heavily.

JR: *In America now, you also have a new form of incarceration at Guantanamo Bay.*

PV: Indeed. America is also in the process of locking itself up and it's no longer a matter of isolationism anymore. It is frankly Fortress America. I wrote the book, *Fortress Europe*, based on the bunkers. The issue of confinement is something I know all about! I spent ten years studying Fortress Europe and the wall of the Atlantic. That was my first book. I made plans of those things.

JR: *Yes, but do you see a difference between the bunkers you're talking about and the bunkers of Iraq?*

PV: It's the bunkerisation of the world! It's the world, including the private fortresses of conformist America. The cities of America are locking themselves up. It's preposterous! Do you know there are 30 million people living in gated cities in America right now? That's half the population of Israel, which is roughly 60 million. I did a special number of the magazine *Urbanisme* directed against private cities.

JR: *What about Saddam's little bunker? What did you think when they pulled this deranged-looking man out of a hole?*

PV: It was rigged! The whole thing was rigged! It was theater, really bad theater. No, no, as I've already said – I was interviewed at the time – it was of no interest whatsoever. It was the same as pulling down the statue of Saddam Hussein. No interest whatsoever. We are waiting for major political acts from America and so far there have been none.

JR: *We've spoken before about the post–World War II work you did for the occupying army – before you got involved in architecture. You said that you not only knew how to use all the weapons of the day but that you also drew ordnance maps for the occupying army in Germany, which was also your education as an architect.*

PV: I was in the general staff of the First Army in Freiburg, in the French-occupied zone. I did the maps for the big interallied maneuvers that would take place in the Black Forest and at the border between the British zone at Stuttgart and the American zone. One of the things I did, for instance – I'm very proud of this – was the staff maps for

General Juin in Baden-Baden. He was the head of the occupied zone and had led the war in Monte Cassino, which led to the whole conquest of Italy. One day my superior said, "Virilio, the maps you've drawn are great, so we're going to transfer you." I used to send off small observation planes, Tigercubs, for surveying the maneuvers in the Black Forest and elsewhere with these automatic cameras. Because I had a certain military intelligence and an ability to represent these situations I was transferred out of the headquarters of the First Army and sent to Baden-Baden. I was pretty happy about that because we had much better digs than the army barracks. Our translator there – I only found this out a few years ago – was Alfred Döblin! Of *Berlin, Alexanderplatz*! When Döblin later died, I was asked to add a word to his obituary, and I mentioned that.

JR: *After your military service ended, was it logical to become an architect?*

PV: Yes, but more important, I had spent most of my childhood in Nantes, which was badly bombed during the war, where thousands died. I saw things in '43 – I was eleven, eleven years old – and I started to write down everything I saw in school exercise books. I called the account *Five Years of War*, and I told what I was living through – I've lost the notebooks since. I was conscious then of becoming a man. At eleven. That's young, don't you think? It's so young! The town was razed to the ground. I saw shocking things, heads cut off, limbs. For a kid of eleven, it was appalling. Terror is the apocalypse for a child. People screaming . . . I found that I was in a philosophical situation, because those who liberated us, killed us, and those who occupied us, lived with us. I lived opposite Saint Jacques Hospital, Rue St. Jacques, in the south of Nantes. Trucks would roll up with the wounded and with corpses all piled up to go to Saint Jacques Hospital. There were German sailors gathering information, German sailors who were wounded, women, and so on – all mixed up together because we'd been bombed by the British. At the same time, I couldn't feel hate for them. You couldn't! We loved them! And we loved the British because they freed us. That's what I meant earlier by "I hate you, but let's stop the bloodshed." I couldn't manage to feel hate. I was eleven years old and I understood that, but at the same time, it was terrible. I was torn in two. I was happy and at the same time I was terrorized. That's philosophical. You become a philosopher in a situation like that. At eleven years of age, you are a philosopher.

When Ernst Jünger died – a great writer – I was asked to write something for one of the German papers because I'd often quoted him. And I said, there is such a huge difference between us, firstly because he's a great writer and I'm not – I'm not a great writer, not like Julien Gracques, who is a great writer – and then, Jünger is a man of war, even a hero, and I'm a child of war. Jünger is a man of war and what a man of war! Iron Cross – thoroughly deserved for '14 and after. I would like to have met him, because he used to read me and I used to read him. I admired him enormously as a man but at the same time, this is the enemy, this is Jerry. Jerry as a hero: the worst! Not a monster from the SS, they're a dime a dozen. Jünger was no monster, he was a great warrior.

JR: *So, you succeeded in escaping from your philosophical dilemma, you were able to turn the tables and become an architect.*

PV: That happened later. I was an urbanist first.

JR: *What did being an urbanist start with?*

PV: It was the bunkers. Without the bunkers, I would not have become an urbanist or an architect. During the 1950s, I got interested in bunkers. I happened to be on holiday by the sea, in Brittany, and you know, there's bugger all to do on holiday – you go swimming, and I'm not much of a swimmer, I always remain a bit of an intellectual [laughs]. Then one day I turned around and found myself looking at a cement blockhouse that reminded me of Aztec forms, Inca forms, a sort of Egyptian mastaba. It interested me. At the time I was interested in painting, but I said to myself, this is interesting. I decided to go into it because, first of all, I'd lived through Fortress Europe; I hadn't had the right to go to the seaside during the war. I lived in Nantes, which was half an hour from the sea, but we weren't allowed to go there, the sea was a forbidden zone. I only discovered the sea with the Liberation, and when I got to the seaside, it was full of blockhouses. For me, it was a bit like finding the statues of Easter Island...a kind of theater, these figures waiting before the sea, immemorial, before the void, and mostly serving no purpose whatsoever.

Suddenly, I developed a passion for these enigmatic objects – in a kind of archaeological way, actually, bunker archeology. So for ten years, I spent all my holidays taking photos. I

bought a good camera, a Leica, and I made a study of the Atlantic. Little by little I realized that this was my world and that I was more of an urbanist/architect than a painter. And there you have it. For me, the bunker and war are linked. The bunker is a metaphor for war.

JR: *What about for life today?*

PV: Today it is a metaphor for the confinement we've been talking about. That's right.

JR: *So you make a direct connection between the two?*

PV: Completely. I can also build, by the way. I've built a church, the Eglise de Sainte-Bernadette (1963–66), in Nevers – Nevers! Remember *Hiroshima Mon Amour*? One of Resnais's greatest films, a wonderful film.

JR: *Wonderful. And so is Marguerite Duras's screenplay.*

PV: Wonderful, wonderful. So when I was asked to submit something to the competition for a church dedicated to Saint Bernadette, I didn't do it just for the sake of it. I hadn't had any formal training in architecture, I never went to a school of architecture. The bunkers taught me everything I knew about architecture. So, first I looked at Bernadette – the grotto in Lourdes. The Lourdes grotto is a bunker. The grotto is the origin of architecture. It is *the* place – the place of birth, the matrix, the source; it's life. And it is protection.

For me, the bunker is a sort of metaphor for the power of destruction and the will to survive. That is, these few meters – three or four meters of cement, seven in submarine bases – that are indestructible, as they say, are for me a sort of metaphor for modern power. So I thought up a church that would have the brutal external look of a bunker – a mass of gray concrete without a hint of stylishness – and an interior in the shape of a heart, of a womb. When you enter it, everyone tells me it's extraordinary, because there's what you see when you first arrive, and then there's what you see when you go in. It was classified a historic monument in March 2000, and now belongs to the town of Nevers.

JR: *The way you describe it, the contrast between inside and outside must be overwhelming.*

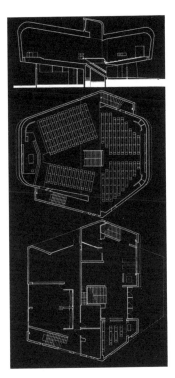

PV: It's the Sacred Heart. Did you know I was consecrated in the Sacré-Cœur? Wait a second, I'll do you my sign [pulls out a pen and begins to draw a heart on the paper napkin]. It's a heart with a cross inside. It's not some priestly gimmick.

JR: *Thank you, Paul. It's beautiful.*

PV: So you see, the church is in the shape of a heart. It's a blockhouse. But in fact, it's the upper ventricle and the lower ventricle. There's the nave for communion, with people moving around and the light coming and setting it ablaze, and there's the nave for confession. Confession meaning profession of faith, not blah blah blah, I have sinned. To confess means to say "I am Catholic, I am Christian." So the two come together, slightly inclined so that everyone can see, because when you are in a level church, you can only see from the first row. So the church is slightly tilted, like so, and you can see the whole assembly.

JR: *How do people like it?*

PV: At first people were horrified by it. Everyone thought it was hideous. In fact, it won the competition for that reason [laughs]. I'm serious. The priest in charge of the project, the Bishop of Nevers, who later became Bishop of Nantes, said, this proposal has aroused so much hate that it's got to be the one I choose. Another bishop from Alsace said, this is a blockhouse, it's hideous! But he was responsible for consecrating it. We were all inside with our families on the big day, I was there with my wife, and it went on for ages because the bishop from Alsace was going all around the church, inside and outside, blessing everything, and the whole time, he kept saying, I don't believe it, it's so hideous. After about 34 times, the resident father, Father Bourgois, a lovely cultivated man, said, listen, I'm the priest of this church, so either you stop carrying on about it or you stop consecrating it; this just can't go on. The bishop shut up and the consecration went ahead. Later, I'm told, the bishop loved it. And everyone else seems to have come round, but you see what I was up against.

I went to Lourdes this year for the first time, and I was knocked out. It was fabulous! Fabulous! It's the first time I've ever been to Massabielle, the grotto. Do you know what that means, Massabielle? It's Basque, the local patois for "old rock," where Bernadette comes from. I went on a pilgrimage with the Bishop of La Rochelle. He was going, and a few of

PAUL VIRILIO, NAPKIN DRAWING.

us decided we'd go with him. Massabielle. I went at night and it was hot, too, over 40 degrees. When I got there and I saw the grotto – I can't tell you! My heart stopped, I knew I was getting near Massabielle. I was stumbling along and gradually I could make out the path Bernadette took to go to the grotto. I kept going, and in the distance, I saw a sort of light coming from the grotto. I can't tell you. It was like love at first sight. I said to my wife, this is where we were born, where we come from.

I've never been to Jerusalem; I've been to Massabielle. At the grotto I felt something I've never felt anywhere before. At night, nobody was there. It was deserted. I felt like crying. I can't tell you. You see: we are Christians. There are no words. When you get up close, it's like a huge heart. Then something else happened. I was a bit behind, so I missed the start of the procession – there's a procession at night. I see an old guy crossing the little bridge opposite Massabielle and I say to myself, he's got to be French, so I go up to him and I say, "Err, do you know where the procession starts?" "Nicht Strachen!" I say, "Oh, you're German?" "Yes, yes," he says. I tell him I'm looking for the procession and he says he understands French very well, but he's afraid that I'm a French soldier, and he was a soldier, so we were enemies. I was once a soldier, I tell him. There is that, but we've moved beyond it. This is no longer the enemy in front of you. And we hugged. And, well, it was fabulous. Perfect. Unbelievable. Just unbelievable. I said to my wife, you realize I stumbled on a German.

You know, Bernadette entered the convent in Nevers – the Sisters of Charity – to hide. She was sick of always being an exhibit, so she said, "I've come to hide myself." The church was supposed to protect her. But in Nevers she was surrounded by all these grandes dames who liked to do good works – the Charity dames were strictly sixteenth arrondissement. One day a lady from the sixteenth arrondissement, probably, very well-to-do, turns up. Bernadette is at the table with the other sisters, and this woman says, now you are going to show me the visionary! Little Bernadette – I think she only measured one meter fifty – is at the table, so they point her out to the woman. And the woman says: "*That's* the visionary? *That!*" And Bernadette says, "Ah, yes, only that!"

What a comeback! What strength! She later went on to say,

why did the Virgin appear to me? Because I was nothing, she couldn't find anything worse than me. If only she could have, but no: it was me. Unbelievable! So strong, so wonderful.

There's another story about Bernadette involving the Germans in the Prussian War in 1870. The Germans had been fighting in the North, and all the wounded German soldiers were bundled off on trains. The trains stopped in Nevers and there was blood everywhere. The soldiers thought, the Sisters of Charity will look after us because we can't cope, there are too many wounded. Bernadette pipes up and says, I volunteer, and she starts tending their wounds. It didn't matter that they were the enemy. She said, these are men, they're soldiers, and she loved them in spite of the fact that they were the German enemy.

That's charity for you! And so, when I saw this German I said to myself, Bernadette has sent him to me! [laughs] You see, I like Germans. They are the wounded.

And that's enough of that. Let's get out of here.

JULIE ROSE LIVES IN SYDNEY, WHERE SHE IS CURRENTLY TRANSLATING PAUL VIRILIO'S *LA VILLE PANIQUE*.

SCENES FROM A CHANGING BEIJING.
ABOVE: BUILDING MATERIALS
MEGAMALL; RIGHT: SHOPPING FOR
PORCELAIN, PLUMBING FIXTURES AND
OTHER BUILDING SUPPLIES. PHOTOS:
RAY FU.

Frank Fu and Qing Fei

Beijing Guide
To Shopping

All of the artwork necessary for decorating your house: the Red Guard, landscape, flowers, the Great Wall, traditional beautires with fans, and so forth. Photo: Ray Fu.

1. Bear in mind: Beijing, like many cities in China, is a city of fakes. There are innumerable buildings in Beijing, and more appear every day, but architecture is rare – an endangered species. For the architect, finding *real* building and furnishing materials is a formidable challenge.

2. Shopping in pairs is always preferable to shopping alone. Salespeople are sincere, enthusiastic, and professional – to the point that they are capable of selling you *anything*. Do they have other options? They have to make a buck or two. We once asked a friend where to buy good cement. He laughed: "Nowhere, unless you own a cement factory."

3. *Huo4 Bi3 San1 Jia1* (compare goods in three stores) is the golden rule of shopping. Throughout Beijing, there are countless shopping malls called *Jian4 Cai2 Cheng2* (Building Materials City). Glance at the price tags, but never buy immediately. The prices marked are smoke screens, designed to fool the amateurs.

4. For the professionals, negotiating is a matter of course. Always begin at half price. On one outing, in search of fabrics, we found a relatively attractive material in a well-known store. The asking price was 58 yuans RMB per linear meter. After half an hour of bargaining, we paid 28.

5. Once we were outside the store, we congratulated ourselves with high fives. Glancing back through the store windows, however, we saw that the salespeople were celebrating, too. The price we had paid still gave them a wide margin of profit.

6. Sixteen years ago we left Beijing for New York, but during the past six years we have found ourselves more and more in Beijing. Beijing yesterday was our hometown, lovely and low. Beijing today is alien – harsh and high. But we still love it. If prices for materials are high, labor is exceedingly cheap, and construction workers and craftsmen are often quite intelligent.

7. As an international construction laboratory, Beijing operates 24/7. Hutongs are knocked down. Towers pop up like mushrooms. The market is borderless. Shopping is endless.

8. Eight is a lucky number in Chinese culture. Good luck. Welcome to Beijing.

Frank Fu and Qing Fei maintain an architecture practice in Beijing and in New York.

Free the architects.

skidmore, owings & merrill

Today, using HP's Tablet PC, architects at the renowned Skidmore, Owings & Merrill LLP can design, sketch, render and revise anywhere. And, with HP's wireless technology, they can share their inspirations instantly from New York to Shanghai. On site or on a plane, these digital tools hike productivity for everyone. www.hp.com/plus_som

+ hp

= everything is possible

When you're attempting to build the newest tallest tower in the world, it can't hurt to have Hewlett Packard running ads featuring your skyscrapers on the back cover of TIME magazine. And the ad's claim is true: more than a year ago, we witnessed Ross Wimer, an SOM designer, using, at HP's invitation, the very Tablet PC the company is touting. – The Log Team

Cynthia Davidson

Scenes from a Less Delirious New York

It still hurts to look at the torn up ground of the World Trade Center site. As steel rises into the skyline on the site of the former World Trade Center 7 building, the forward momentum of rebuilding Lower Manhattan seems unstoppable. But that is simply stating the obvious. Since the day the Twin Towers fell, there has been no looking back. There has also, I would argue, been no looking forward.

In the New York of the late 1920s, a moment that Rem Koolhaas extols in his 1978 book *Delirious New York*, there is great hope for the future of the skyscraper because the skyscraper embodied the idea of the future, a realm for "new and exhilarating human activities in unprecedented combinations." Like the Futurists of their day, the planners of the 1920s reveled in speed, noise, and congestion that could be generated by a one-block one-building formula. This formula made the fabric of New York, with the exceptions of Grand Central Station, Rockefeller Center, and the then modern idea of the World Trade Center.

But where the Plan Commission of the 1920s endorsed the skyscraper because it symbolized a modern New York, today the planners of the World Trade Center site want to restore the square footage of the Twin Towers to the 16-acre site not for symbolic or cultural reasons but rather for purely economic ones. This approach is said to be for the benefit all of New York City. But should this particular site really bear sole responsibility for repairing the economy of Lower Manhattan? For it also clearly benefits the Port Authority of New York and New Jersey and its leaseholder, the developer Larry Silverstein, whose economic well-being is tightly bound to leaseable floor areas.

Hence, when Governor George Pataki formed the Lower Manhattan Development Corporation after 9/11 – adding a third political interest to the development process – he charged it with the task of rebuilding a commercial center that would bring 24-hour life to downtown. This was a pragmatic agenda, not a symbolic one. Media hailed the new oversight committee as a sign of forward momentum necessary to quickly heal the wound in the city. The corporation set about planning to restore streets once blocked by the plinth

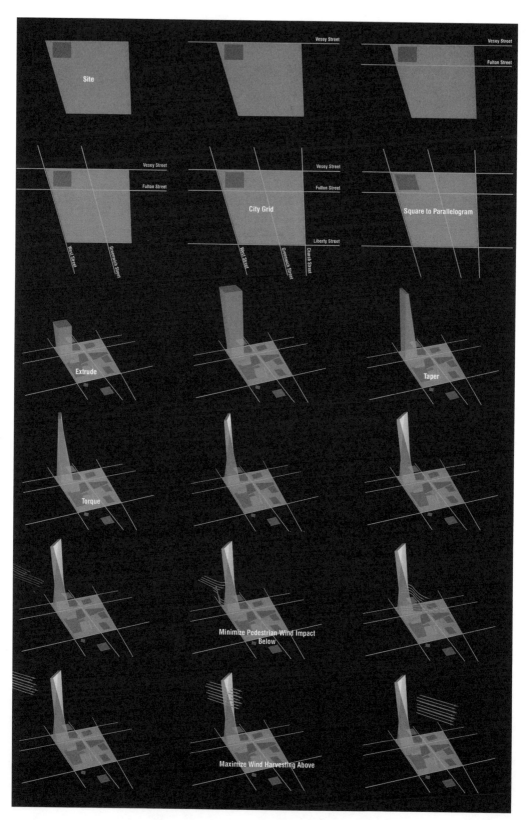

Site

Vesey Street

Vesey Street
Fulton Street

Vesey Street
Fulton Street

West Street
Greenwich Street

Vesey Street
Fulton Street

City Grid

Liberty Street

West Street
Greenwich Street
Church Street

Church Street

Square to Parallelogram

Extrude

Taper

Torque

Minimize Pedestrian Wind Impact Below

Maximize Wind Harvesting Above

Skidmore, Owings & Merrill, design development of the Freedom Tower. From top to bottom: site/streets, streets/building and square to parallelogram, extrusion and tapering, torque, minimizing impact of wind on pedestrians, and maximizing wind harvesting above. Image courtesy SOM.

1. Cited in Rem Koolhaas, *Delirious New York* (New York: Oxford University Press, 1978), 100.

2. Koolhaas, *Delirious New York*, 100.

of the WTC on the premise of easing traffic flow in Lower Manhattan. Those same streets also create city blocks for single skyscrapers, a return to the patent formula that "is" the real estate grid of New York. The LMDC also called for "a tall symbol(s) or structure(s) that would be recognized around the world" on the grounds that the loss of something very tall could only be replaced by something very tall, if not taller. Media and politicians concurred. With these two acts, New York did not move very far from the position of the Plan Commission of the 1920s, which said:

All accept the skyscraper as something which serves human needs, but judge it differently as to the value of this service. All know that it has become the dominant feature in the structural composition of large American cities. But is it also to be the dominant feature in the social organization of all urban life in America? If we attempt to answer this question we would have had to go deeper than we have dared to go in the Regional Survey and Plan.[1]

Deeper too, apparently, than the LMDC in a very different time has dared to go or, for that matter, even speculate on. In fact, the finesse of the LMDC's process of public meetings, control of information, and use of web site opinion polls seems to have thrown the possibilities for "deeper" critical thinking or criticism into disarray.

The LMDC design competition held in 2002 was supposed to generate a symbolic project for the WTC site, but today the competition seems like an elaborate cover-up to which both media and politicians tacitly agreed: media because of their critical silence about the process; politicians because symbols don't buy votes. In the year since Daniel Libeskind won the commission for the WTC master plan — in which he proposed four new towers for the site, among other buildings — there is little evidence that questions about the symbolic value and meaning of the city in terms of its architecture are still being asked of this development. In 2003, Libeskind's proposal was a popular favorite but not a critical one. The symbolism of his Freedom Tower, with its 1776 height and "outstretched arm" like the Statue of Liberty, was emotion-based kitsch that scored high in public opinion polls and then won the governor's vote. But as the project was changed by the Port Authority, Silverstein, and his architect, the critics who could not originally support Libeskind's plan found themselves not only unable to defend the competition-winning master plan but also complicit with its substitute: with what is now a purely technological feat still called the Freedom Tower. Except for the name, the kitsch is mostly gone, and the public, curiously apathetic.

Those who could criticize the current tower – now scheduled for groundbreaking on July 4 – are mostly silent.

As Koolhaas writes about 1920s New York, "Everything may be questioned within the framework of the Regional Plan except the Skyscraper, which remains inviolate. Theory, if there is to be any, will be adapted to the Skyscraper, not the Skyscraper to the theory. 'We will have to accept the skyscraper as inevitable.'"[2]

Nearly 80 years later, the WTC redevelopment only reaffirms what has become a rote response to building in the city. The height of a tower still says power. Never mind that big corporations' dispersal of assets and work forces to multiple urban and suburban locations is not a temporary response to terrorism, or that the centerless world of the Internet suggests that the city is becoming a series of networked "centers" of many sizes. When a vertical commute takes longer to complete than a high-speed link that accesses the world at the touch of a key, does the tower become obsolete? Are the supertall towers being built in developing countries casting New York in old-fashioned shadows? Or is the tower in Manhattan simply a real estate investment too great to refuse? Even the Museum of Modern Art will acknowledge, if not endorse, the continuing impulse toward the skyscraper when it opens the exhibition "Tall Buildings" this summer.

Though the WTC site, with its railway connections and air space could sustain another Pan Am building – for Koolhaas, Pan Am was the ultimate in mixed-use skyscrapers – instead the supertall Freedom Tower will gratuitously (and for a price) bear broadcast antennae for the movement of information. No wonder the *New York Times* critic Herbert Muschamp, who only two years ago led a charrette to embolden proposals for the site, has now confessed sympathy for the "cop-out" position to rebuild the Twin Towers as they were rather than follow the development path currently suggested. It speaks not only to the failure of criticism to effect critical thinking but also to the collusion of media with politics and business interests.

Investment is vitally important to the well-being of a city. But when I look south from my kitchen window at night, I too wish the white lanterns of those towers were still illuminating the night sky; not because I want to go back, but because criticism and, it seems here, architecture seem to have lost the ability to spark the public imagination, to open the public, the politicians, the bankers, and media to the idea of shrugging off the easy rote response in order to ask how we might go deeper to conceive of a different, and better, future.

A DIAGONAL STRUCTURAL GRID, OR DIAGRID, ENCIRLCES THE PERIMETER OF THE SUPERTALL TOWER AND SETS IN MOTION THE TWISTING OF ITS FORM. PHOTO COURTESY SOM.

ABOVE THE OCCUPIED PORTION OF THE BUILDING, THE TWISTING GEOMETRY BECOMES A SYSTEM OF CABLES SUPPORTED BY TWO CIRCULAR STRUCTURAL CORES. PHOTOMONTAGE BY DBOX; IMAGE COURTESY SOM.

SCENE ONE

"At Last, Skyline Begins to Heal," the *Daily News* reported in December 2003 when the model of the Freedom Tower, designed by David Childs in collaboration with Daniel Libeskind, was unveiled. In March, while lecturing in Rome, Childs said, "I felt it was our duty to take [Libeskind's] master plan and accept it and try to make it better." This "duty" included revisiting Libeskind's tower to find something more "simple and forceful to be the final spire that would recapture the skyline of downtown." The resulting torqued and tapered structure is no longer Libeskind's "shepherd with a crook," as Childs called it, but a tower with an "abstract and powerful dynamic relationship" to the Statue of Liberty. At the same time, the "asymmetrical spire at [the] corner, that literal translation of the arm of the Statue of Liberty . . . has now been called the bayonet of the building," he said – clearly indicating his continuing desire to change it.

Michael Arad and Peter Walker, "Reflecting Absence," the winning entry in the international design competition for a memorial remembering the September 11, 2001, attack on the World Trade Center. Right: Santiago Calatrava, PATH Station design for the World Trade Center site, seen from the west.

Scene Two

In February, the *New York Times* asked in a front-page story, "Still not satisfied with the pool-filled voids on the site of the twin towers? Count your blessings. It could have been . . ." suggesting that the jury for the WTC memorial design competition had "saved" New York from a worse fate than what is now to be built. When the jury paired housing architect Michael Arad with landscape architect Peter Walker in the final competition phase, it also, perhaps unwittingly, circumvented Libeskind's proposal for a 30-foot-deep depression alongside a "heroic" slurry wall – itself a memorial proposal. In deciding to build Arad's scheme, the jury pushed the cultural buildings proposed for the site away from the memorial and then softened the site with Walker's tree plantings – which looks a lot like design by jury. The LMDC said that Lower Manhattan draws seven million tourists a year, and that the memorial will draw more. But the dwindling number of visitors to the memorial to the victims of the Oklahoma City bombing begs the question, who and what are these memorials for?

Scene Three

When Libeskind first presented his WTC scheme in late 2002, he gave a certain voice to the ineluctable horror that had haunted New Yorkers since 9/11. But as time passed, his terminology seemed to lose luster. When his proposed "Wedge of Light" became the site of the Port Authority's new commuter PATH train station, no objections were heard. Instead, the station, designed by Santiago Calatrava, was hailed as embodying that wedge of light, its glass and steel roof letting natural daylight into the commuter/retail space within.

The media greeted Calatrava's bony extravagance with overwhelming approval: "Wow." But the bird-in-flight concept that also served for his museum project in Milwaukee seems a mixed metaphor here. In fact, it is no more than an ostentatiously engineered Venus's-flytrap to lure commuters and shoppers into its subterranean commercial spaces.

Scene Four

In the interim, New Jersey commuters now use the temporary PATH station designed by Port Authority architect
Robert Davidson. As trains pull into the rebuilt platforms on
bedrock, commuters ride up escalators to a concrete deck
that spans the site nearly to Church Street at the east. There
a fashionably utilitarian steel canopy announces "World
Trade Center Path Station" in large letters. The walkway
from train to street is also the closest visitors can get to being
on the site itself. Curious tourists find themselves standing
quietly, looking, perhaps taking a photograph. The station
now feels like the real memorial, still raw, unpolished, tough.
But it too will disappear.

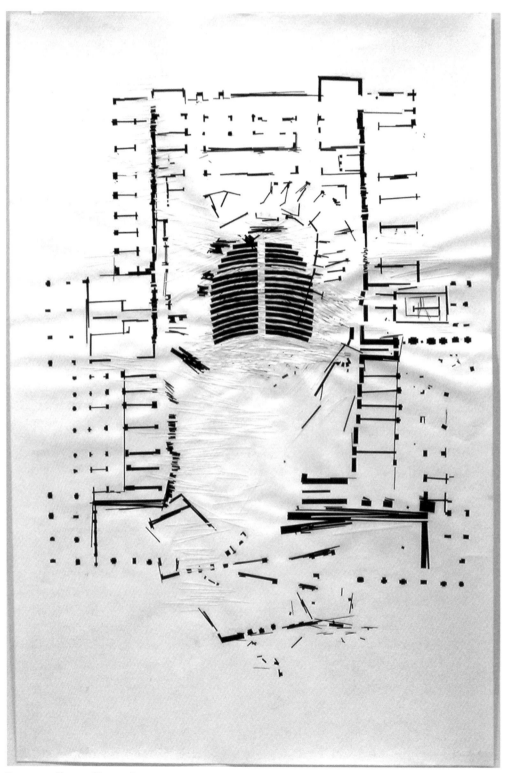

GUILLERMO KUITCA, *WEINER STAATSOPER*, 2003. MIXED MEDIA ON PAPER,
57 1/2 BY 38 1/4 INCHES (146.1 BY 97.2 CM). COURTESY OF THE ARTIST AND
SPERONE WESTWATER. KUITCA LIVES AND WORKS IN BUENOS AIRES.